# Indoor Soccer

# Indoor Soccer

## Tactics, Techniques & Teamwork

### Evert Teunissen
*Photography by Hans Heus*

**Sterling Publishing Co., Inc.**
New York

## Acknowledgments

I would like to thank all of the players of the Dutch national league (especially "Mr. Indoor Soccer," André Van der Leij) for their kind help in taking the photographs that illustrate this book. Thanks to Hans Heus, who also contributed greatly to these photos, to Will Jansen, from the Olympic Sports Center in Wijchen, and to *Zaalvoetbal Magazine* for the additional photos. Finally, my thanks to Ray Schoenmaker for statistics and to Jacques Stoppelenburg for his information on the national indoor soccer teams.

Translated by Natalia Tizón

Edited by Elizabeth Kaufman

Designed by Joan Columbus

**Library of Congress Cataloging-in-Publication Data**
Teunissen, Evert.
    [Zaal voetbal. English]
    Indoor soccer : tactics, techniques & team work / Evert Teunissen.
        p.   cm.
    Includes index.
    ISBN 0-8069-9714-1
    1. Indoor soccer.   2. Indoor soccer—Rules.   3. Indoor soccer—
Coaching.   I. Title.
GV943.9.I6T48   1997
796.334'8—dc21                                           96-39981
                                                             CIP

10  9  8  7  6  5  4  3  2  1

Published 1997 by Sterling Publishing Company, Inc.
387 Park Avenue South, New York, N.Y. 10016
Originally published by BV Uitgeversmaatschappi, Triion, Baar (Holland)
under the title *Zaal voetbal*
© 1995 by Evert Teunissen
English translation © 1997 by Sterling Publishing Co., Inc.
Distributed in Canada by Sterling Publishing
% Canadian Manda Group, One Atlantic Avenue, Suite 105
Toronto, Ontario, Canada M6K 3E7
Distributed in Great Britain and Europe by Cassell PLC
Wellington House, 125 Strand, London WC2R 0BB, England
Distributed in Australia by Capricorn Link (Australia) Pty Ltd.
P.O. Box 6651, Baulkham Hills, Business Centre, NSW 2153, Australia
*Manufactured in the United States of America*

Sterling ISBN 0-8069-9714-1

# Contents

# Foreword

As President of the NZF (Dutch Federation of Indoor Soccer), it is an honor and a pleasure to write the foreword for this basic guide to the game.

After a personal meeting with the author, Mr. Teunissen, I discovered that our ideas on the sport are virtually identical. Few people can speak so clearly and with so much conviction about the sport as he.

Indoor soccer began in our country approximately twenty-five years ago. Today, there are more than 24,000 clubs playing indoor soccer and 1,000 conventional soccer clubs have an indoor soccer division.

With over 300,000 players, more people participate in indoor soccer than in any other indoor sport in this country. Sadly, opinions concerning indoor soccer within the KNVB (Royal Dutch Soccer Association) are so varied that the Dutch press rarely reports the development of this sport. Indoor soccer is growing and unstoppable. Although conventional soccer suffered a setback in popularity in recent years, the interest in indoor soccer continues to rise, particularly among our young people.

Mr. Michels, the KNVB's technical director, has recently come up with the idea of training young players four-on-four in a reduced playing field in a game that comes from conventional soccer. Indoor soccer is now an alternative for male and female players. The game is evolving so rapidly that boys and girls will have a choice between conventional soccer and indoor soccer. The NZF will have to make sure that the rules for indoor soccer are not a copy of those in conventional soccer, because indoor soccer is a different sport.

Coaches must try to ensure that indoor soccer continues developing technically and tactically. They should emphasize technical play. We should not allow indoor soccer to become a chess game. That would be extremely bad for its development.

We must all work together to take this sport to the highest levels. The NZF will try to lead the way.

I sincerely recommend this book on indoor soccer, and I am sure that it will make a valuable contribution to the sport.

J. Wierts (NZF President)

# Preface

For the fans, indoor soccer is a separate sport, but some people do not believe this yet. "Why talk about differences when the only real one is a roof?" they ask.

In fact, there are many more differences. Indoor soccer has fewer players (which means fewer technical possibilities), smaller goals, a smaller ball, less than half the outdoor playing area, a different type of playing surface, and specific game rules. With this book, we intend to make the difference clear, not only for the men and women who play it, but also for anyone interested in the sport.

Indoor soccer is a young sport. It started less than twenty-five years ago. Not many international competitions are held yet, although the UEFA (European Soccer Union) and FIFA (World Soccer Association) have tried to unify the rules of the sport. This is not an easy task.

Many of the players, coaches, and delegates are inexperienced. Most come from conventional soccer and most are volunteers.

Approximately 300,000 people play indoor soccer in the Netherlands. Half of them play in a league (organized by the KNVB, or Royal Dutch Soccer Association), and the other half play the sport in sporadic tournaments, for recreational purposes.

I hope that this book will be of help to the increasing number of players. I have tried to clarify the axiom of "indoor soccer, a different sport" and to offer possibilities for coaches and players to help their teams with techniques, tactics, and physical fitness. I must admit that I have intentionally avoided talking about physical fitness in great detail.

Evert Teunissen

# What Is Indoor Soccer?

Indoor soccer is very simple. All you need is a sports arena, a couple of goals, a ball, and some lines marking the boundaries. The game is a refined form of street soccer. Actually, it is the primitive elements of street soccer that have made indoor soccer so popular.

Indoor soccer has gradually gained fans, becoming very popular in the United States. Recently both American and European media have become interested in it. However, a comparison between indoor and outdoor soccer only extends to the most general aspects of teams of players seeking to control a ball primarily with their feet. In the details these are two different sports using a different number of players, as well as different field measurements, balls, and even shoes.

American indoor soccer, played on an artificial turf surface in an oval playing area, has more in common with European indoor soccer, played on a hard surface in a square playing area, than outdoor soccer has in common with indoor soccer. Unfortunately, the UEFA refers to indoor soccer as "also soccer, but indoor instead of outdoor and where the same rules apply."

"In bad weather," the UEFA continues, "the outdoor fields are not in condition to play on. It is too cold in the bleachers and this is why a sports arena is a good alternative. Only half the number of players are required because the field measures about half of the outdoor one, but something is better than nothing."

The new sport of indoor soccer can hardly accept this explanation. Most professional outdoor soccer clubs prefer playing indoor soccer, as the Americans do, on an artificial turf, a felt-like carpet that is easy to slide on.

Indoor soccer uses six players (including the goalie) on a side. It uses bigger goals that have a net on the back. In the United

States, where indoor soccer is widely accepted, arenas have playing areas that vary from 165 to 200 ft (50–60 m) long by 100 to 115 ft (30–35 m) wide on artificial turf rounded at the corners, and with a seating capacity of about 10,000 spectators. The possibility of scoring is so great that goalies can barely show their potential.

The European playing areas for indoor soccer by their nature have led to some differences from the United States. The Netherlands, for instance, is a country with quite a few sports arenas; while they are generally good facilities, a typical playing area is only 130 by 65 ft (40 by 20 m) with a 6-ft (2-m) perimeter, and a seating capacity of 500 to 1,200 spectators. These facilities do not have permanent artificial turf since this would require a bigger playing surface. The Dutch also have several larger sports arenas on which to play one or more matches, but this depends on the installation and removal of artificial turf as quickly as possible.

In a letter to all affiliated soccer federations at the beginning of 1987, the FIFA expressed its opposition to using artificial turf in indoor soccer. In the secretary general's opinion, the

first FIFA trial tournament proved that indoor soccer games do not need artificial turf. Therefore, the FIFA recommended that regular competition and tournaments not use this kind of turf. However, the differences between European and American indoor soccer persist.

Another area of conflicting standards for the sport arises because world soccer experts do not agree about the rules of the game. The biggest controversy regards the body contact rule. During the three trial tournaments played in Hungary, Spain, and Brazil, experts expressed different points of view: "Sliding should be possible to a certain extent. A shoulder push makes the game more physical, and soft pulls and pushes are not necessarily a problem. An unintentional trip can be overlooked, and the delay in restarting the game also occurs in conventional soccer. If things get complicated, the referee can make use of the yellow and red cards, because, above all, the numerical equity has to be preserved."

Experience has proven that many things must happen to achieve numerical superiority. A yellow card is no longer so easy since the coach can replace the player who received it. Only red cards cause a numerical difference, but only after a serious foul.

Even though we use masculine terms when we speak of indoor soccer, we should take women's indoor soccer very seriously. On this and the previous pages, we can see two players from the Dutch team with good ball control and great concentration.

# Evolution of the Sport

Indoor soccer is arguably the most popular sport in the world. While other sports measure their popularity by the number of fans, indoor soccer continues to see the number of players increase.

Although this sport is heading towards general recognition, many obstacles stand in the way, especially those coming from conventional soccer. Each day it is clearer that we are dealing with different types of soccer and that the two types should coexist instead of opposing each other.

International indoor soccer competitions have already begun. Lugo, Spain, held an international tournament in 1985 in which Belgium, Italy, Spain, and the Netherlands took part. An unofficial world championship in Budapest, Hungary, was won by the Hungarian team. The United States, Peru, Brazil, the Netherlands, Belgium, Italy, and Spain also took part. A second experimental tournament took place in La Coruña, Spain. It ranked Spain, Belgium, Bra-zil, the Netherlands, the United States, Peru, Italy, and Portugal. Other tournaments have since followed.

Conventional soccer began in 1863. In the English colleges of Rugby, Harrow, and Winchester, people played soccer with a round ball. Rugby (which took its name from the British city) used an oval ball. That same year, the Cambridge and London associations founded the Football Association.

One hundred years later in Holland, Kas Stuive founded the Helder Indoor Soccer Organization (HZVO) to see how it would work and to keep players together in the winter months. Stuive's competition started with teams from summer soccer tournaments, company teams from the Den Helder area, and soccer clubs that belonged to the KNVB in that North Holland province. It worked. In fact, it worked so well that after one year, the number of clubs doubled. The organization reported to the KNVB, which did not acknowledge the increasing num-

A scene from women's soccer.

ber of players and popularity of indoor soccer. However, because of pressure from the Den Helder outdoor soccer team, the KNVB decided to intervene. The professional outdoor soccer clubs wanted to ban its players from indoor soccer since many of them had already started to play on various indoor soccer teams, making some team members rivals, which caused problems.

After more than two years of dialogue, the KNVB accepted

Indoor soccer resembles street soccer because the players can dribble and practice one-on-one situations. The players in this picture and on the next page are good examples of this.

indoor soccer. Actually, it really didn't have a choice because the HZVO was legally recognized by that time.

On June 30, 1967, an indoor soccer commission met in the Netherlands with representatives from all organizations of this sport and the KNVB. The first action of this commission

was to survey the twenty KNVB divisions.

The main questions were:

1. Is indoor soccer played in your division? How often? Do you hold competitions or just sporadic games?

2. Do you consider the development of indoor soccer a threat to conventional soccer?

3. Do you think that indoor soccer should only be played during those periods when conventional soccer is not played?

4. Do you think that indoor soccer should be restricted to certain age groups?

5. Do you thing that indoor soccer is a completely different sport from conventional soccer and, therefore, that the KNVB should not deal with it? Even in the future?

The opinions of the divisions concerning indoor soccer were as follows:

All the divisions agreed that indoor soccer was not a threat to conventional soccer. Four of them thought that it should be restricted to periods when conventional soccer was not played.

Two stated that it should be considered a different sport and that the KNVB should not deal with it.

In many countries, the construction of sports arenas in the 1960s and 1970s accelerated the growth of indoor soccer. More conventional soccer players felt attracted to the "small team game" where the goals and systems depended on the pleasure of the game. Also, body contact was not allowed.

This made it possible to dribble the ball, beat the opponent, and take pleasure in scoring points. Outdoor soccer has deteriorated in some ways. The game has become more physical because of the necessity of eliminating the opponent in some competitions. In order to avoid losing, teams created more defensive systems even if this harmed the pleasure of playing the game. The game didn't encourage initiative, and creativity became dangerous. In fact, soccer became boring for the players and even more so for the spectators. The game lost appeal for young people, and they turned to indoor soccer because

it was still played like street soccer.

## Street Soccer

Actually, indoor soccer still has much in common with street soccer. The players can dribble, no one interferes, and the rules don't take away the fun. Dribbling, passing the ball, shooting, beating your opponent, and above all winning require great skill with the ball.

## A Welcome Compensation

Rinus Michels said that indoor soccer would not be a substitute for outdoor soccer: "Too poor, lacking in variety and space to effectively move the ball." At the same time, Michels stated that "especially for young people, this type of soccer will be a good balance for street soccer, which has been lost. The 'game' is better with players who have technical ability because they must control the ball within a small area with hard surfaces. This requires great ball control. The game is dangerous when played with too many rough players. These players often lose the ball, and the physical well-being of their opponent is in danger. Indoor soccer is a good alternative for young players during the winter months and a good way of learning better individual technical skills and ball control.

"Indoor soccer could not only be a good alternative for young players during the winter months, but also an important step towards becoming a good outdoor soccer player."

Street soccer used to be played with a small rubber ball in fenced-in school yards after school. Before the game started, players would choose sides by playing the children's game of paper-scissors-rock: four children marking the goals, dribbling, trying combinations, wanting to win, using the system of play based on running ahead without interruptions. All of this was street soccer.

# Specific Ball-Handling Techniques

January 1987 has a special place in the recent history of indoor soccer. At that time, teams from Europe participated in the Third European Clubs Championship in Maastricht, Netherlands. The Hoboken of Antwerp won the first championship in 1985. In Viterbo (Italy), the Belgians defeated the Kras Boys from Volendam, Holland. The next year the championships were in Italy again. In Rome, the Drei Keunige club from Maastricht defeated the Belgian champion, the Hasselt, winning the European Cup for the Netherlands.

The winner of the Third European Clubs Championship was the Naestved IF from Denmark, a traditional soccer team using its winter break to stay in shape by playing indoor soccer. They laughed at all the indoor soccer traditions and broke the attractive systematic game of their opponent in the finals. The result was 7–0 for the Danes.

**Technique, speed, and performance:** The Danish players achieved their huge victory with these three principles and with the help of great physical conditioning. Using continuous substitutions, they exhausted their opponents.

Such an offensive, aggressive game is equally adaptable to American as well as European indoor soccer provided the players develop their technical abilities.

## Technique, Speed, and Performance

Indoor soccer is a sport for players with technical skill who like to control the ball, to fake out the opponent, to score goals through individual play, and to work with teammates to score. Controlling the ball is important in indoor soccer.

The speed with which players receive and pass the ball must be as great as possible, requiring technical and tactical control.

The indoor soccer diagram on the next page shows the relationship between technique (and tac-

Players constantly search for solutions to defensive problems. The concept of "opportunity" dictates that a player's actions depend on moment-by-moment individual play. Here, the defense (5) knows that his opponent is trying to make him lose his balance by feinting.

The photo on the next page shows how to control the ball with the inside of the foot behind the support leg. This can also fool the opponent.

tics), speed, and performance.

1. TECHNIQUE
   Dribbling, passing, ball control

The photo on the next page shows how to control the ball with the inside of the foot be-hind the support leg. This can also fool the opponent.

2. SPEED
   Thinking and acting

3. PERFORMANCE
   Tactical aspects and scoring

## Major Techniques

Dribbling, passing, and ball control are the main technical elements in indoor soccer. The instep and head shots are less frequent when trying to score goals. This is why in indoor soccer practice, for both individuals and the group, players must work on situations oriented towards the goal.

**Dribbling**, feinting, accurate ball passing, increasing speed, cutting, and turning require much practice and regularity until the player's skills become automatic.

**Passing** the ball to a teammate is a specific action requiring execution speed, ball speed, and accuracy so that the ball reaches the teammate's feet at the right moment and in the same direction he is turning. Players need to be able to do this with the inside or outside of the foot.

**Controlling** a ball that reaches the player at a fast speed requires the player to reduce the speed of the ball (but not stop it) and take it in one movement to an open space to continue the game. The player should be able to do this with both feet and with both the inside and outside of the foot.

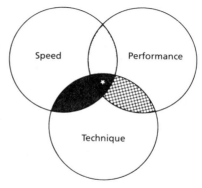

Speed

Performance

Technique

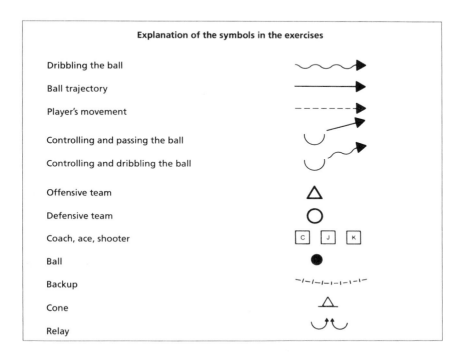

Explanation of the symbols in the exercises

| | |
|---|---|
| Dribbling the ball | |
| Ball trajectory | |
| Player's movement | |
| Controlling and passing the ball | |
| Controlling and dribbling the ball | |
| Offensive team | △ |
| Defensive team | ○ |
| Coach, ace, shooter | C J K |
| Ball | ● |
| Backup | |
| Cone | △ |
| Relay | |

# 1. Dribbling the Ball

Indoor soccer is played in a relatively small space (often with six to eight players in a 65 by 65 foot (18 by 18m) area, so players must pay much attention to dribbling the ball.

Define a 65 by 65 foot (18 by 18m) square with cones. Every player has a ball and calmly dribbles within the defined area. The coach observes the behavior and movements of the group. He can make observations about using both legs, using both the inside and outside of the foot, or about moving the ball at a consis-

tent pace. He gives instructions and demonstrates what he wants the players to do. He also explains that the players can do it another way as long as the other way puts them in an advantageous position.

The coach should choose only the most important instructions, depending on what he sees in the drill. Coaches should not give more than two or three instructions per practice because too many interruptions or too many corrections can diminish the fun and make players (especially the young) lose initiative.

### Instructions
- Take the ball to where there is more room.
- Gradually look less at the ball and try to see where there is some empty space.
- Take the ball to an empty space as quickly as you can.
- Use the leg and side of the foot closest to the ball.
- Make yourself faster by lowering your center of gravity and using your arms for balance.
- Make sure that the foot carrying the ball is not too tense because you could lose contact with the ball, and your opponent could steal.
- Keep the ball next to your foot so that you can turn to protect it, preventing your opponent from stealing it.
- Slow down so that you can see the new situation.
- After a couple of quick moves,

Photos 1 through 13 show how to help players improve their ball control skills. Here, the players show how to reach the one-on-one situation in a methodical way without opposition. The focus of this exercise is on moving the body behind the ball in order to catch the opponent off balance. The player needs to slightly lower his center of gravity. He uses his arms to provide good balance. The player must keep the ball very close to his foot.

1

2

3

4

5

6

7

8

9

10

11

12

13

slow down and continue dribbling calmly.

- Increase speed towards the open spaces at the sides.
- Make sure that you are still within the defined area, using the lines on the playing area even during practice.
- Use the inside or outside of your foot to stop the ball so that you can turn inside the line and continue in the opposite direction, controlling the ball.
- Try this exercise of stopping and turning in the defined area when your teammates are approaching.
- Do it slowly at first and do not look at the ball too much.
- Try it with your other leg as you become better.
- Use the whole area and choose the best solution, once with the inside of your right foot and once with the outside of your left foot.
- Control the ball or change sides with the sole of your feet.
- Try to keep the ball rolling with each movement. Try not to stop it.
- Pass the ball behind your support leg. Use the inside of your right foot behind your left leg and then dribble it out with the outside of your left foot.
- Make sure that you bend your

support leg sufficiently and that your body is slightly above the ball. Use your arms for balance.

These are some of the most important exercises. The coach must observe, analyze, give instructions, demonstrate, motivate, and especially try to keep the game fun.

### One-on-one

The one-on-one is an important feature in indoor soccer, especially from an offensive point of view. Dribbling against an opponent, beating him, and learning a situation of numerical superiority requires technical ability, practice, and repetition with different roles and drills. The one described above is a good example of one for a small area. Don't forget the coach's instructions: "You can also do it this way, although you should choose your own solution."

### Drills

Another possibility is to form one or two frontal rows.

Each player advances by dribbling the ball between the lines, trying to beat the defensive player. Dribbling requires all kinds of feinting movements and passes. The coach may dictate these or the player may simply react to the situation.

## Example

The player takes one step to the left. He flexes his support leg (the left one) a little, leans for a moment on the left leg, and then shifts his body to the right. At the same time, the player moves the ball to the right with the outside of the right foot. This type of exercise is very helpful in learning how to beat an opponent. Finish the exercise with a shot on goal.

The players may also work from the center line to the goal line and vice versa, meeting halfway, thus reducing the area where the passes take place. A player can look at the ball, but he must be careful not to bump into the other players. The exact moment to pass the ball depends on the space, the circumstances, and the position of the rest of the players. The player must pay attention to both the ball and the imaginary opponents.

Players can also practice one-on-one against a very active defender. Use two goals for this exercise. The definding player must try to get the ball back and to keep the other player from scoring. When a player loses the ball, he becomes the defender. However, when one player scores, the other continues defending.

## Two-on-one

This is a good exercise. Two attacking players work together against one defender. They can pass the ball to each other or play a one-two combination, switching places or not, running after the ball or waiting for it in an empty zone. Relays can also provide good practice (see "Relays" below).

Two-on-two, three-on-two, three-on-three, four-on-four, up to five-on-five or even full matches are very interesting and produce real game situations. Players must practice attacking against increasing opposition, starting with numerical superiority (four-on-two, four-on-three, and three-on-two), and then with equal numbers (four-on-four, three-on-three, and two-on-two) with or without limitations. To achieve maximum contact with the ball, alternate players and only shoot at the goal after the relay, a successful wall, etc.

Photos 1 through 6. Actual practice in a small area must be a daily routine for indoor soccer players, especially for young ones. This is an excellent way to develop total ball control until their skills become automatic. In these pictures, the players follow instructions from their coach. They dribble against each other between four cones, each time with a different objective.

1

2

3

4

5

6

### Observation

Repeat all of these drills using a limited space that depends on the number of players, their ages, and their technical level.

Six to ten years—50 by 50 feet (15 by 15m) for twelve players.

Ten to fifteen years—40 by 40 feet (12 by 12m) for twelve players.

Sixteen and over—30 by 30 feet (10 by 10m) for twelve players.

Ball handling (controlling, dribbling, and passing) must become automatic:

- during warm-up sessions
- as a form of exercise with or without opposition
- in play or competition

In this way, each warm-up session can end with a play. The players have prepared their muscles for it. Players must also be mentally prepared to better deal with game situations.

### Drills with a Hunter

Here's a good example of a practice in a 40 by 40 foot (12 by 12m) area defined by four cones.

All players except one have a ball at their feet. The one without it, the hunter, must try to get one by touching another player's ball as the players dribble through the defined area.

- The hunter tries to steal one

or more balls and to kick them out of the square.

- The player who loses a ball then tries to steal a ball.
- He must first try it with the player who took his ball. If that fails, he can try to take another.
- Whoever touches, shoots, or recovers the most balls in thirty, forty-five, or sixty seconds wins.

For a more difficult drill, let two hunters devise their own strategy.

### Observation

The players unconsciously have a lot of contact with the ball. When practicing with one or two hunters, the pace will constantly change. Moving the ball using both feet and both parts of the foot will become almost effortless. After all, the player does not want to be touched and has to defend himself. Stopping, turning, and pulling back will help improve ball control.

The players must quickly find solutions, not only technical

ones (a kind of ball control), but also tactical ones (which direction). Physical condition is important here, and the coach must respect the work-rest ratio, depending on each player's level of play. Exercises are a way to improve ball skills, tactical vision, and physical capability. This is why coaches must be imaginative, creating different ways of practicing, establishing limitations, and introducing variations.

### Variations
- If you keep the ball high, juggling it with your feet, thighs, and head, no one will steal it.
- Do not play the ball more than three, four, or five times. Continue dribbling.
- Look at the potential passes that you can make to the four players outside the area. You can make one-two combinations (wall).
- You cannot make two one-two combinations in a row with the same player.
- After each one-two combination, you must dirbble around one of the cones.

### Relays
Continuing the game is not always possible, and, in some cases, the player must keep the ball. This will slow down the pace of the game and increase the risk of losing the ball. Relays can be good solutions to these problems.

Relays are very appropriate for indoor soccer because of:
- fewer possibilities of shooting from a distance
- little space to dribble
- very tight defense

Under such conditions, it is easier to shoot on goal. The unexpected chances of scoring increase. Players can maintain a faster pace for a longer period of time, and the risk of losing the ball is low.

A good relay can have a surprising effect. You can even pretend you are going to do one. In a relay, a teammate approaches the player who is dribbling the ball, takes the ball with the inside of his foot, and continues dribbling or passes it to a teammate who is in good position at that moment.

### Relay Exercises
Situations that surprise and increase the pace are situations of numerical superiority, such as two-on-one, three-on-two, and four-on-three, which open gaps in the opponent's defensive system.

The third player is also important. During the relay, this is the player who looks for a position and signals for the ball to shoot or to pass to a fourth player who is approaching.

- Player 2, on the right side, dribbles towards the center.
- Player 3, on the left side, also moves to the center. He receives the ball from Player 2.

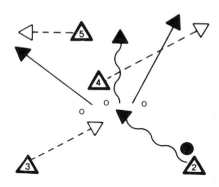

The possibilities for Player 3 include:

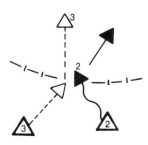

Player 2 is a backup.

- pass to Player 4, in the center, who takes up a new position
- pass to Player 5, the advance player, who takes up a new position
- dribble alone towards the position left by the advance player

The possibilities for Player 2 (faking a relay) include:

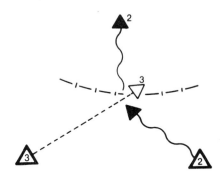

Player 3 is a backup.

- pass to Player 5, who takes up a new position
- pass to Player 4, who takes up a new position
- dribble alone to the position left by the advance player

The exercise offers many more possibilities and solutions.

35

A good coach will be creative, considering the capabilities and specialties of his players. The coach determines the execution, the "where" and "how" to take a new position, and how to take advantage of the opponent's defensive mistakes.

In the cases above, Player 5, the advance player, and Player 4, the one in the center, take the defense with them. Player 2 or Player 3, whoever has the ball, can advance, covered from behind by the other player.

Player 2 dribbles towards the center.
- Player 4, in the center, approaches the ball, takes it, and passes it directly to Player 3, on the left side, who takes the appropriate position.
- Player 3 can pass the ball to Player 5, the advance player, who takes up a new position, or to Player 2, on the right side, who takes up a new position. Eventually, Player 3 can go to the position left by Player 5.
  Player 4 is a backup.
- Player 2, on the right side, dribbles towards the touchline. After establishing visual contact, he passes the ball to Player 5, who receives the ball at his feet.

- Player 5 stops the ball and continues the play by dribbling towards his half of the field.

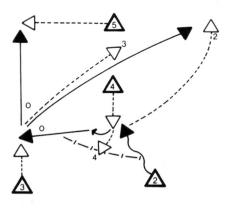

Player 4 is a backup.

- Player 4, in the center, takes the ball and dribbles to the position on the right side in the offensive area.
- From there, Player 4 can pass to Player 3, who is approaching on the left side, or to Player 2, on the right side. He can also continue dribbling towards the goal line to continue the play from there.
- In this play, Player 5 is a backup.

### Observation 1
When either Player 4, in the center, or Player 5, the advance player, dribbles, a simulated relay occurs, and the advance player maintains possession of

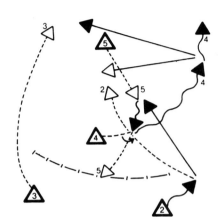

Player 5 is a backup.

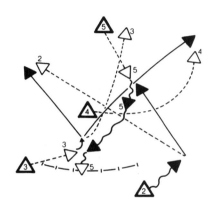

***Observation 2***
After an attempted relay, Player 5 maintains possession of the

Player 5 is a backup.

the ball. He can pass to Player 3, on the left, who takes up a new position, or to the outside to Player 4, who takes up a new position, or to Player 2 on the right side, who is approaching through the center of the field.

ball and dribbles towards his half of the field. Player 3 can take the ball and pass it to Player 4, who takes up a new position on the outside, or to Player 3, on the right side, who takes up a position towards the left side. Then Player 3 takes up a position in the center.

At first glance, these are not simple routines. They are examples of how to make indoor soccer more appealing. Relaying the ball is a good way to break a tight defense. It is also attractive because it gives plenty of opportunities to move with and without the ball.

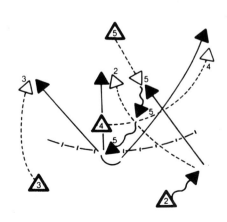

Player 5 is a backup.

Possession of the ball is important in indoor soccer. This picture of a great instep kick shows the importance of performance. The numerous spectators prove that the technique, speed, and performance of indoor soccer make it an attractive sport to watch.

The relay is especially important in indoor soccer. The playing area is relatively small, and most players occupy half of the playing area. The players in pictures 1 through 3 show a relay in which one player stops the ball under his foot and then continues running into an empty zone, opening it up. The other player takes the ball and continues dribbling. During practice, a good coach must explain the advantages and disadvantages of the relay and work to achieve good collaboration, communication, and understanding among the players.

1

2

3

4

In the relay in photos 4 through 6, the player stops the ball and follows with a direct pass. Another player watches the ball when his teammate passes it.

Photos 7 through 9 show a common mistake in this type of relay. When a player stops the ball under his foot, the ball should not slide backwards, or the player receiving will have to change direction and may be caught off balance.

5

6

7

8

9

### Points to Pay Attention To in a Relay

- The player who dribbles must make the defender aware of his approach.
- The teammate taking part in that play must make clear with eye contact and by increasing his speed that he is ready.
- The player who initially had the ball must continue moving towards an empty space or backing up.
- The player who receives the ball must know the next potential situation. He can either pass or keep the ball.
- Relays are means to achieve a situation of numerical superiority or an unexpected combination, but they are not objectives.
- During practice, a good coach can underscore the advantages and disadvantages of relays and focus on good teamwork, especially collaboration and communication. Starting with efficient ways of taking up new positions, the coach can make relays and attempted relays the main issue. Tactical practice can consist of working in situations without opposition, with numerical inferiority, superiority, and ending with a five-on-five complete game with goalies.

### Drills and Competition Plays

Practice three-in-one, four-on-two, three-on-two, and four-on-three drills in a limited area, such as half of the playing area which you have clearly defined so everyone understands. Emphasize the relays.

Let's analyze the three-on-one as an example:

In both halves of the playing area, which are 60 by 60 feet (20 by 20m) each, two groups (one in each half) compete against each other.

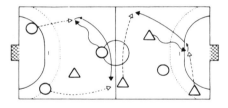

- Award one point for each relay.
- Award one point for each relay immediately followed by a pass.
- Do not award a point after a relay until a player dribbles to the outside of one of the cones.
- Deduct one point from the offense if the defender takes the ball.

**Note:** Change the defender after one, two, or three minutes.

- Substitute players so that all players have an opportunity to play.

- Substitute another offensive player of the same team who plays in the other half.

You can also use these exercises playing four-on-two, three-on-two, and four-on-three. The more players and the smaller the numerical superiority, the more difficult the practice situations will be because of the reduced space and the increase in defensive players.

You can also play three-on-three or four-on-four games in different combinations:

- without a goalie
- with a goalie
- with or without shooters on the touchline or the goal line

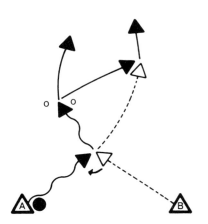

Try this in pairs along the field:

Player A dribbles forward along the side, and Player B picks up the ball along the length of the field.

Player B continues dribbling and passes to Player A, who takes up a position.

Player B can also try to score after dribbling.

Instead of a relay, you can just simulate one where Player A contines with the ball and ends the play or passes to Player B, who takes up position.

Try this with groups of three along the field:

After the relay along the length of the field, pass to Player D, the advance player, who takes position, or to Player C, who is approaching on the side. Instead of a relay, you can simulate

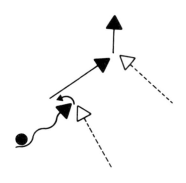

Players may only take a shot at the goal after a relay or a relay and a direct pass.

You can also practice exercises to improve the relay in pairs or in groups of three.

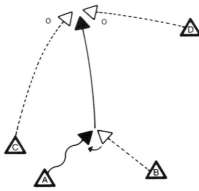

one, so that Player A continues with the ball and ends the play or passes to one of the two players who take position.

When trying this in pairs or groups of three, the coach has to clearly indicate the organization. This exercise works with or without cones, benches, and goals. You can also create a form of competition with defenders.

The photo above shows a successful relay. After the relay, the player can pass the ball directly to any player who requests it.

### Indoor Soccer Is a Different Sport

It requires a specific type of ball control since the circumstances are different from conventional soccer. The playing area and ball are smaller, and the rules pro-hibit body contact. Playing in a reduced area requires getting used to. The instep kick is more frequent when shooting, and players pass the ball with the inside and outside of the foot. The series of photos shows ball skills.

In the photo above, a player shows how to stop the relay with the outside of the left foot. His teammate waits for the moment to receive the pass.

1

Passing a ball just received requires a great deal of concentration. The moment of passing is critical in controlling the direction and height of the ball.

Timing and the movement of the leg are extremely important (Photos 1, 2, and 3).

2

3

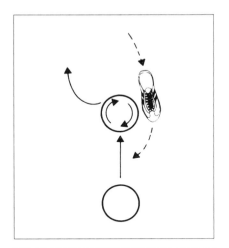

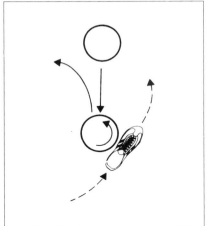

When moving the ball with the outside of the foot and giving it spin, the player must concentrate, calculate the path, and follow through with the leg.

Adding spin is a useful technique in indoor soccer. The foot must touch the ball softly. The outside of the foot gives a spin to the ball towards the outside, and the inside of the foot makes it turn to the inside. The object is to pass the ball around the opponent to a waiting teammate.

Photos 1 through 7. The player can handle the ball differently, receiving it with a smooth movement without controlling it. The player lets it roll between his legs, turns quickly, and then carries it away. In this case, the speed of the ball is not important. The player lowers his center of gravity, uses his arms to help with balance, and makes a short pass appropriate to the situation.

1

2

3

4

5

6

7

The player can also receive or approach the ball by feinting, shifting the body to one side, and pulling back the support leg. Concentration, timing, a low center of gravity, balance, and good foot work are all important. Even if the player isn't very fast, he won't lose the ball (see photos 1 through 5).

4

5

6

Photos 6 through 10. Approaching a ball to play it at a 90-degree angle to its trajectory requires a lot of concentration, a low center of gravity, timing, eye contact with the teammate taking up position, correct leg movement, and follow through after kicking the ball.

51

Although heading isn't used very frequently in indoor soccer, players are scoring more goals with this technique every day. Practicing this is similar to conventional soccer. The landing varies. The players in photos 1 through 4 show the importance of the proper way to land hands and feet on a hard surface. The arms should act as struts, and this requires exercising the ankle and elbow joints. The shoulder joints absorb the impact on the ground.

1

2

3

4

Chipping the ball can be a good way of passing it over the defender's feet. Faking out a goalie who leaves the goal or who slides down by crossing with a chipped ball is a superb shot (photos 1 through 3).

1

2

3

A player needs good body control to come from the side, over the ball, cut it, and dribble it inside the circle (photos 1 through 4).

## 2. Passing and Ball Control

In indoor soccer, most players use instep kicking for shooting on goal. The field is actually too small to make big instep passes. The longest kick is no more then 115 to 130 feet (35 to 40m) in a counterattack play. The front part of the foot hits the ball from underneath, creating a slight spin so that the ball turns in the opposite direction, stops in the air, and falls gently at the feet of the advance players. Some players specialize in this technique.

Concentration when passing.

Players use chip passes to change the play. These passes need to be practiced regularly.

In each of the corners of the field—A, B, C, and D—there are three players. One in A makes a chip pass with the left foot and continues walking towards B. A player in C receives the ball, carries it towards D, and passes it to another player who makes a chip pass with the right foot to B, where a player receives the ball, takes it towards A, and passes it on.

Left-handed players must start in A and B, and right-handed players in C and D. Since the use of both feet is a big advantage in indoor soccer, players

need to practice with their "bad" leg. When possible, they should practice with two balls at a time. The play begins with a player from A and one from D. They should pass the ball with the outside and inside of both feet and even with the heel rather than with the instep.

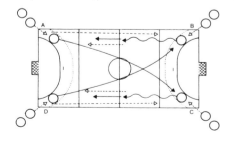

When we talk about passing the ball, we also need to talk about controlling it. Controlling the ball in a certain direction and running with it are two technical skills that go together. The field is smaller, the defenses are more pressing, and the game is faster. Controlling the ball must be automatic, without looking at it. The player must be able to anticipate the next move.

Passing and controlling the ball are technical skills that players practice in small areas by using a lot of movement. Three-on-two and four-on-three practices and three-on-three and four-on-four games are very appropriate for this. They develop the ability to position, pass, and take a new position. The player only needs to control difficult balls or exercise control when first-time kicks are not possible or desirable. In all other cases, the player should pass right away.

### Drills

The diagram illustrates an exercise in which the ball needs to be played at first touch, and in which two players must move constantly. Seven players (including the goalie) form a circle and pass the ball to players across from them. Three players are defenders and try to steal the

ball. When they steal it, they switch roles. The objective is to pass the ball at first touch except when passing through the center. In order not to give any opportunities to the defense, the ball must travel very fast. The constant movement of the players before and after touching the ball is also important in this exercise.

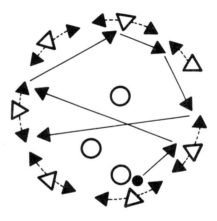

Players must move with the ball to the left or the right, bring it close to them every so often, carry it with their feet at moderate speed, and try to fake before shooting. If they want to change the play, they pass to the teammate across from them and change direction and speed. The defensive players will lose contact between themselves and won't be able to recover the ball.

Players rarely use the instep shot in group play. More frequently, they chip the ball to change the play with the toe slightly under the ball and the body slightly bent back. They use the instep shot to score goals.

In photo 1, a player shoots the ball with an instep kick to the goal. Photo 2 shows a ball at half height with perfect body balance and the toe of the support leg pointing in the direction of the goal. In photos 3 and 4, we see how a player "squeezes" the ball, and another player shows the elegance of indoor soccer when volleying.

1

2

3

4

For the group game (see photo below), the pass with the inside of the foot is best. If possible, practice the pass with both feet. Players can also use the outside of the foot. Here, two players practice direct zigzag passes at maximum speed.

5

Photos 1 and 2 show that even in official international competitions, players use technical shots on goal. A player with a strong instep shot and a player with an outside instep shot prove this point. Women's indoor soccer is as exciting as men's.

1

2

Continuous movement before and after touching the ball is important. Move with the ball to the left or to the right. Bring the ball closer to you and even let it run between your feet. Try faking direct shots.

Indoor soccer is a good alternative for young players during the winter months and an interesting step in the development of a conventional soccer player. It provides opportunities to improve technical skills, to work on creativity, and to practice balanced movement. Thanks to indoor soccer, many players have become better outdoor players.

## 3. Shooting

Indoor soccer is a sport that should be fun to practice. This is why drills, ball control exercises, and exercises to improve the group and positions game should not take too long. Players should spend most of their time practicing plays and in matches. This is a better way to learn than practicing specific skills. For example, use a three-on-three game with four or six shooters (K on the diagram) outside of the playing area. They should be on the touchlines and the goal lines. In this kind of practice, the better the technique, the better the shot will be. Also, this will make one-two combinations (give-and-go) more functional.

The player takes the ball behind his leg and practices passing and controlling it with the outside and inside of his foot, moving the ball behind his support leg with the left foot as well as with the right foot.

### Possibilities for the Three-on-Three Position Game

- Practice individual defense
- Award one point for each pass to a player who shoots on goal
- Award one point for each one-two combination
- Practice with two goals
- Shoot freely on goal
- Shoot only after a one-two combination through the shooters
- Practice with two goalies

The individual defense during this type of practice can:

- Increase technical skills
- Use the shooter to avoid the defense
- Noticeably improve the position game

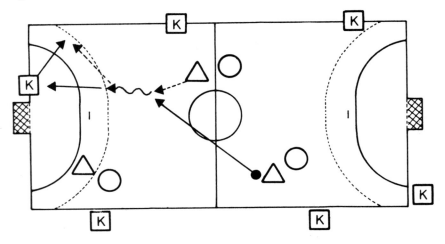

In a three-on-three game, you can add four or six players on the outside of the playing area. They stand on the touch-lines and goal lines. The players on the playing area make continuous one-two combinations with these players. The better their technique is, the faster the shot will be.

- Improve physical conditioning
- Exert a positive influence on the concept of competition

A good coach needs to make sure that this practice is not too intense. Overly intense and aggressive practice can have a negative effect, making the objective of shooting depend on a position game that is too fast. The relationship between work and rest is vital in role changes. In this type of practice, the six players off the playing area now take part in the three-on-three game and vice versa. The coach will immediately notice if any players are tiring because the pace of execution slows down and the players lose concentration.

### The Role of the Shooter

This is the player who is either waiting for the ball or approaching it, acting as a middleman in a teammate's individual play (one-two combination) or in combination with two teammates (one-one-two combination). The shooter can be Player 5, the ad-vance player; Player 4, in the center; Player 2, on the side; or Player 3, returning from the opponent's half of the field. In most cases, it is Player 5, who, with a defender behind his back, returns the ball to the same player who passed it to him (a one-two combination with direct passes, the third one being the longest).

### A Good Shooter Must

- Return the ball quickly at a precise speed
- Put little or no spin to the ball
- Make the correct choice between the one-two and the one-one-two
- Hide what he is going to do
- Fake before shooting

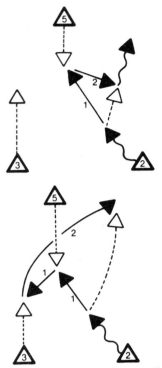

working towards both sides, from goal to goal, back and forth. This is a way to fill in more of the playing area, which is something that both the player who passes and the one who shoots must be aware of. They need to know the exact moment of each action of the play, and sometimes one of the two will have to keep the ball.

• In the final stage of this exercise, you can use one or more defenders. You can also use an individual game to complete the play.

The coach observes, accompanies, and corrects both the technical execution and the tactical performance in each part of the exercise: playing or keeping the ball, determining the execution speed in one-one-two combination and in one-two combinations, with or without

• Return to the game after shooting, either in the offensive or defensive group

### Exercises

The group is in two rows, one on the left side and one on the right side. The players alternate taking off from each row. They dribble, and then one of the two advance players receives the ball and they take turns shooting. After the one-two combination, the shooter continues ahead and shoots on goal.

To practice the one-one-two combination, use this system:

• Later, practice this in waves,

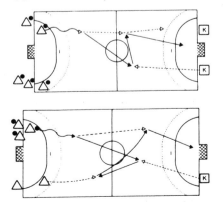

goalies, shooting after receiving, and shooting directly.

### Observations

Make sure that the player who is ready to shoot is not too close to the goalie or the shot may be too hard. If the player is too close, he must use the inside of his foot. Another option is to remove the goalie. You can also mark the area from which the players should shoot.

## The Goalie in Indoor Soccer

The ideal indoor soccer goalie must:

- Look at the ball at all times
- Protect the short angle
- Be fast enough to reach a wide angle
- Maintain his position and not go to the floor too fast
- Have an incredibly high reaction speed with his legs and feet
- Keep his knees close together
- Arch his knees, hip, and trunk slightly
- Keep his hands on both sides of his hips, elbows slightly pointed to the sides
- "Push" with elbows and forearms
- Maintain concentration
- Provide fast tactical defense
- Exhibit proper competitive spirit

Some goalies play actively, too. In general, however, their participation is limited. Although at some point the goalie can have a positive influence on the game, that is up to him to decide. He can do it to help with the offensive play (numerical superiority) and provoke the opponent's advance player or to prevent him from going directly back to his half of the playing area.

Most teams have perfected tactical measures against an advanced goalie who is eager to take part in the offense play. This is why most goalies do not participate in the offense.

The goalie may hold the ball in his hands, but this is not necessary (1). Keeping the area around the goal empty through quick actions is more typical of indoor soccer. He needs to be fast on his feet to reach a wide angle. Incredible foot and leg reflexes (2). The indoor soccer goalie must always look at the ball (3), bend at the waist slightly, and always concentrate (4).

3

4

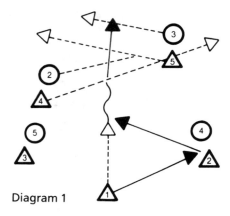

Diagram 1

- The goalie may hold the ball, although this isn't a good idea. In indoor soccer, you want to keep the goal free by quickly kicking the ball out.
- Although the goalie may fall on the floor, he should try not to, especially not too fast.
- He should keep his knees together (not let balls go between them) and, when falling, block with the outside of his leg (less risk of injury).
- The goalie needs to move quickly from post to post to stop balls coming from both left and right.
- He should pass the ball immediately to a teammate, using a direct and quick pass.
- The goalie should pass with the inside of his foot.

Diagram 1 shows how the goalie can advance without problems. Player 4 and Player 5 back up, far away from each other; Player 2 and Player 3 are on the sides. Player 2 and Player 3 of the opposite team cover Players 4 and 5.

Diagram 2 shows how Player 4, in the center, intercepts the advancing goalie. Player 4 forces the goalie to pass in a risky situation.

However, the goalie's main role is to defend the goal. Anything he can do to help the offense without creating any risks is a plus.

### Practice for the goalie
Indoor soccer goalies do not have an easy time practicing. The floor is hard, the ball is small, and opposing players can shoot hard from a very short distance.

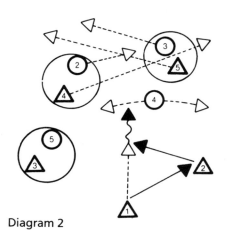

Diagram 2

# Drills and Specific Applications

## Possibilities

What indoor soccer needs is an attractive way of playing. Whether playing on the typical American artificial turf surface or in the slightly smaller, square hard-surface playing area in the European style, the game needs its own tactics and approaches distinct from the very different game of outdoor soccer. People outside this sport may find systems and tactics difficult concepts, being more comfortable speaking of specifics like execution speed and efficient movement, which are easier to connect with ball control and with achieving a certain level of teamwork in the game. Recreational players may find such discussion takes pleasure away from the sport.

The more technical skills a player has, the more he can run with the ball, look at his teammates and opponents, and make correct decisions for the continuity of the game, whether that is to run with the ball or to take up his own position.

### *Look, Think, Decide, Execute*

The decision needs to be made in a fraction of a second. The tactic (both individual and team) is actually a mental process.

Picking players for the team (five basic players and substitutes) depends on the system of play. The system depends on the players available and their abilities. This is the starting point for a coach to form a team that plays successfully.

The coach designs the system. The group of players must know how to execute that system of playing, must have technical ability, and must have good eyesight.

### *Basic Formation + Concept = Style of Playing*

In other words, the style of playing is the basic concept for every team. You can identify it by the choices and positions of the players, among themselves and towards their opponents, and by each player's duties, aimed at achieving greater efficiency.

One of the definitions of playing style is the ability to adapt, which good teams show by changing styles of play whenever necessary.

The team must be proficient in different styles and able to make variations during the game. We will mention three styles. The basic formation starts with:

- one goalie (Player 1)
- two side players (Players 2, 3)
- a center player (Player 4)
- an advance player (Player 5)

Criteria for selecting a style include:

- Which players are available?
- Who controls the ball?
- What is the goalie doing, participating in the game or staying behind the line?
- Which system of plays does the team have?
- What is the score?
- How important is the match?
- How much time is left?

No matter which system the coach selects, two concepts are very important: You must score goals and prevent the opponents from scoring, and you must attack when you have the ball and defend when you lose it.

## Tactical Training

In playing position, the use of the free space is vital. You have to use the space given up by the opponent efficiently.

The offense must be properly organized. The defense will have less chance against an orga-

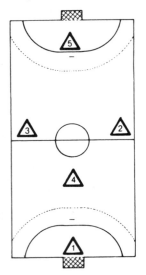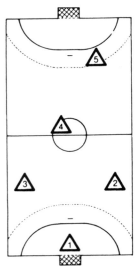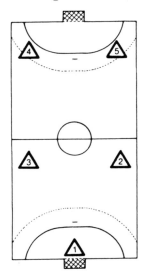

nized attack from the opposing team. They will lose contact between their players—because the offense changes positions, and each defender will have to run after one attacking player.

We differentiate between the following concepts in tactical training:

- Position-taking
- Position-changing
- Individual game
- One-two combinations
- One-one-two combinations
- Relays
- Superiority versus inferiority

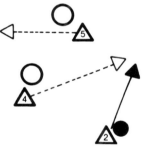

### Position-taking

The player without the ball looks for the open area to elude the defense and receive the ball.

### Position-changing

The players who have taken positions exchange them to surprise the defense.

### Individual game

If the defenders cover the attacking players as they take or change positions, the player

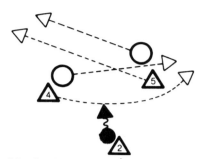

with the ball will have to keep it and continue the attack.

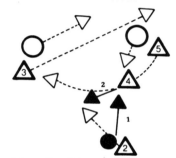

### One-Two Combinations (Give and Go)

The player with the ball passes it to a teammate while he takes position. The player who receives the ball immediately passes it back to the same player that he received it from.

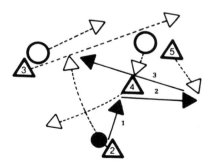

### One-One-Two Combinations

In this situation, the ball does

73

not return to the player who passed it initially, but to a third player who also has taken up position.

After both the one-two combination and the one-one-two combination, the player can pass the ball to a second or third player to continue the play individually.

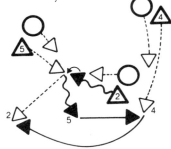

### Relays

When the defense is man-to-man and pressing, a good solution is for a teammate to take the ball. One player will run to the teammate who has the ball and take it from him, either to pass or run towards the goal.

But of course, there are other solutions.

### Superiority Versus Inferiority

You can create situations of numerical superiority to make the attack easier. This happens when you take a good position and change plays—during the individual game—in one-two or one-one-two combinations, or even in relays.

We have already mentioned superior situations, such as two-on-one, three-on-two, and four-on-three, in which players can execute in an organized manner. This organization can be in reduced spaces, in an empty space, using goals, with shooters on the touchlines and/or the goal lines, touching the ball many times, with few touches (two or three) or playing directly (first-time kicks).

Let's take the two-on-one position game as an example.

This is a good way to practice making one-two and one-one-two combinations and to start the individual game at the right time.

Player 2 dribbles the ball towards the opposing Player 5 and passes to his teammate, who returns it to Player 2. Now he passes the ball to Player 5, who will return the ball.

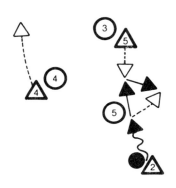

You can also practice relays and individual games:

- without ending in a goal
- completing the play with a goal

### Observations

- The player without the ball picks it up from behind the other player if the opponent is covering him.

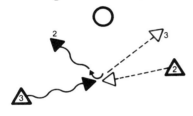

- The player without the ball picks it up in front of the other player if the opponent is covering the position.
- The player without the ball pretends he will pick it up, but he lets his teammate continue dribbling.

### Two-on-One with Five Players

Players 5 and B work together in different ways:

- Sideways pass, taking up position
- More sideways passes, taking up position

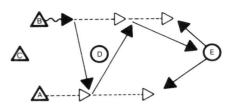

- Receiving, dribbling, playing; receiving, playing, and if possible playing first-time kicks
- Receiving, dribbling, and making a relay, changing places

The defensive Player D tries to make teamwork between Players 5 and B difficult. They should play towards Players C and E, and Players 5 and B can earn points.

### Variations

Players C and E play in different places after every pass they receive, with the offensive Players 5 and B respectively, depending on who passed.

The areas where Players C and E play change after a certain period of time, for example with Player 5 and D or Player D and B, etc.

### Observations

In the position game, the tactical development, efficient movements, taking position, timing, speed of the ball, and the player's decision to control, pass, or dribble the ball are fundamental.

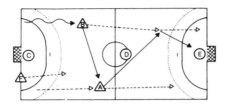

### Two-on-One with Six Players and Two Goals

After completing the play with a goal, both offensive Players 5 and B continue towards the goal line. The goalie, Player E, joins defensive Player D and starts a new offense towards the opponent's goal, where Player C is already defending and Player F is the goalie. Players D and E play two-on-one against Player C and try to complete the play. After this, both continue to the goal line and Players C and F will now play two-on-one with Player 5 as a defender and Player B as the goalie, and so on.

### Observations

The coach watches closely and encourages good development. If the team's tactical execution is poor, with repeated mistakes, he should stop the exercise and correct the situation.

He can direct the defenders to be less active, allowing a better understanding of the exercise, or he can give the attackers more chances to be creative.

In competition, after the defender has recovered the ball, he can immediately organize a counterattack with his goalie. The surprised attacking players cannot defend, and one of the two players in the opponent's goal becomes a defender.

The coach can also emphasize in the one-two combinations, relays, and individual games (one-on-one)—completing the play by taking a shot on goal.

### Other Position Plays

Players can practice three-on-one, four-on-two, three-on-two, and four-on-three games in the same way and with the same organization.

For example, you can use a four-on-three situation with eight players (one defender can be the goalie) and also with twelve players by adding a break, during which four offenders can practice at the highest possible pace.

For three-on-three and four-on-four situations (numerical equality), you can use the same rules. Basically, it is a matter of using the open area efficiently, moving well with or without the ball, and finding gaps in the defense to increase the chances of winning.

In numerical superiority situations where one group has only one more player than the other (two-on-one, three-on-two, and four-on-three), the direct game (first-time kicks) is not easy, and players must retain the ball at certain moments (when no players may move freely). In this case, a relay can be the solution.

In a numerical superiority situation where one group has two more players than the other (three-on-one, and four-on-two), different possibilities exist.

**When playing three-on-one,** move towards the right and left sides.

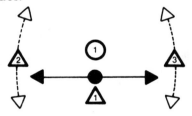

**When playing four-on-two,** move towards the right and left sides and the center.

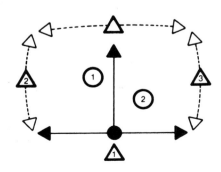

*Observations*
The goal of this exercise is to play the ball directly. The way in which the players take position determines which player will receive the ball.

When playing first-time kicks, the plays must be technically well executed (well-timed passes), especially when the defense is aggressively pursuing the ball.

In terms of physical conditioning, position plays are an excellent way to increase the capacity of movement, running speed, and physical endurance.

The coach should observe and select the right moment to take an active break. This usually occurs when the quality of execution diminishes or when the players lose concentration because they are tired.

An active break can be, for example, passing the ball to each other.

**In four-on-three situations,** we are in a real match scenario, especially if we consider that the opponent must play with one fewer player, since that player has, say, been expelled from play for two to five minutes.

Players need to play the width and length of the playing area, to occupy both sides of the field, and to have an advance player

77

In four-on-three (numerical superiority), the coach must be sure that his players use the width and length of the playing area, occupy both sides of the field, and play close to the touchlines. The players must move the ball at the highest speed possible

and, if the situation allows it, kick directly (first-time kicks). This requires a level of great technical skill. The players must use the inside of the foot to gently keep the ball within the boundary lines.

close to the opposing goalie. They must play the ball at the highest possible speed (depending on technical skills) and, if possible, make first-time kicks.

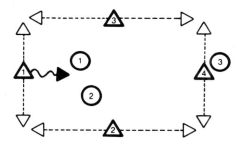

**Problem 1:** When in a position of numerical inferiority, you must pull back towards your own goal. This will reduce the opponent's playing area and the possibility of a deep pass.

**Problem 2:** The offense's lack of patience can make them kick a deep pass too early. They risk losing the ball and being counterattacked by the opponent. The advantage of superiority then becomes a disadvantage.

Priorities in each situation of numerical superiority (normally four-on-three) must be:

- Maintaining patience so as to score at the right moment
- Preventing the opponent from taking the ball because your team made the wrong pass at the wrong moment

Numerical superiority in in-door soccer should be an advantage. The players need to practice this situation regularly, establishing a healthy rapport among the players, coordinated by one player. The rules of the sport penalize players for certain infractions with a temporary expulsion that creates a situation of numerical superiority.

### Example of Numerical Superiority

Player 2, on the right side, and Player 3, on the left side, pass the ball to each other once or several times while they wait for the advance player, Player 5, to take position at the right moment behind his opponent. Then, they make a deep pass and Player 5 can score. In this play, Player 4, in the center, must stay away.

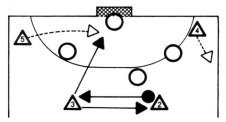

With the same starting position as in the first possibility, Player 5 stays on the left side, Player 4 stays on the right side. Side Players 2 and 3 pass the ball to each other, and then one of them shoots to surprise the defense.

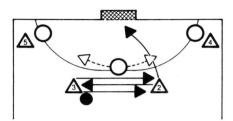

With the same starting position as in the first and second possibilities, Side Players 2 and 3 pass the ball to each other. At the right moment, Player 2 jumps over the ball and Player 4 approaches for a shot on goal.

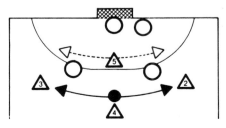

Player 5 can also move in front of the goal—from left to right and vice versa. Player 4 and side Players 2 and 3 pass the ball to each other, intending to play it at the right moment with Player 5.

The deep pass to Player 5 can come from either Player 4 or

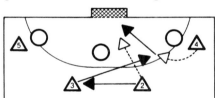

from one of the two wing players. These three players are constantly moving around his position—sideways to the right, sideways to the left, a little ahead, and backwards.

Player 3, on the left side, can dribble the ball from his half of the field, looking for the defender, who is standing closest to the center. He will try to set up a one-on-one (individual play), or he will play sideways towards the back where, for example, Player 2 will try to score.

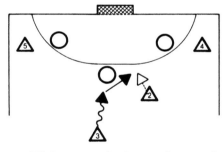

This example shows the possibility of a relay or "backheeling." These are unexpected solutions, but at the same time not simple at all. Remember that performance should always be more important than form.

### Observations

Patience is an important virtue for each situation of numerical superiority. A guided practice (oriented by the goalie) is very important.

Apart from the relays, backheeling is a good way to confuse a very close defender. Player 3, covered from behind by Player 2, sees his teammate running. Backheeling may be his solution.

Other possibilities and situations will require different decisions. Apart from instructions from the goalie, at least one player must make decisions and establish some guidelines.

Team rapport, regular players, and substitutes are necessary. A situation of numerical superiority creates an advantage that should produce results. If the attacking team is winning the match, they will want to kill time by keeping the ball moving among their players. This is not very desirable, but it is understandable during the last four minutes of the game. The other team must recover the ball despite any inferiority. This offers possibilities for the attacking team to even the scores.

## Games with Three-on-Three and Without Goalies (Four-on-Four)

Playing a complete game provides satisfaction. During practice, playing a match is an excellent exercise. Players can do this at the end of a series of technical, tactical, and conditioning exercises with or without goalies.

However, you'll also want to use training matches to develop or improve the style of play, to achieve a rapport among the players, and to avoid mistakes in the offensive and defensive organization. The coach should accompany, stop, and correct the players during the match to practice specific situations.

"Stop for a second, hold the ball, and listen to me," he might say. "This is not going as it should. When Vic has the ball on the left side, Peter must open to the left, totally in the left corner. Then Vic can make a long and fast pass on the left side to Peter and advance through the field. Then Andy must change position from the center to the right corner. Now Peter can play in front of the goal to Andy, who gets there at the right moment, or he can return the ball to Vic.

"Jeffrey offers rear coverage in this quickly executed combination. We will try this play once more. John, Bob, and Henry, you offer little resistance, and Marty, who is the advance player, causes little trouble. Is this clear? Now, Vic, you can start the attack."

The coach tries to use the qualities of each of his players to improve the quality of the game and the team. He suggests a possibility until the moment the ball reaches Peter, who is in the left corner. Peter must now make a decision. Should he play the ball in front of the goal, return it to Vic, who is advancing, keep the ball, dribble, shoot, pass in the goal area by backheeling to Vic, or let Vic take the ball?

The coach suggests possibilities, but he expects the players to come up with their own solutions because situations always change.

The coach also can add an objective to the exercise:

As an objective for the exercise, the coach can decide that in a three-on-three match they can only score by heading the ball when they receive a pass from one of the corners.

- Move a lot without the ball
- Play directly (first-time kicks) whenever possible
- Use one-two combinations
- Use one-one-two combinations
- Use relays
- Complete the play

Exercises with an objective can be useful for both groups of players, although they are primarily for one. The other group can defend individually or the advance or center player can recover the ball. If they lose the ball, they quickly return to their own half of the playing area.

We've already mentioned playing with shooters in the corresponding chapter of this book. Playing with a "wild card" can also be a good way to make these practice matches attractive and varied. The wild card is a neutral player (wearing a different jersey) who always plays with the group that has the ball, to create a situation of numerical superiority. In other words, a three-on-three situation will always become a four-on-three. This is a job that makes the at-tack game easier and compli-cates things for the defense, which is always numerically inferior.

Both teams have three players and one goalie. The neutral player (wild card) always plays with the team which has the ball. When one group loses the ball, the neutral player switches to the other team. Therefore, the teams constantly alternate numerical superiority.

The coach can make the group play with four small goals in the corners to improve the vision of the players. Bringing the game to the corner, where there are fewer defenders, helps develop teamwork among the defenders. If the team loses the ball, the same number of defenders must guard each of the two goals in the corners or at least the same number of attackers.

Finally, the coach can rule that the players may only score by heading the ball (without goalies) directly from a pass from one of the corners or from a chip pass after controlling the ball with the chest.

After observing his players, the coach can impose his own objectives on the exercises and help the group really enjoy the game.

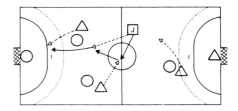

## Three-Zone Drills

Three-zone drills can be very useful in indoor soccer practice. Although the forms—(one)-two-two (with two side players and two advance ones) and (one)-one-three and (one)-three-one (one center player and three advance players)—suggest a two-field game, modern indoor soccer is mainly played with three lines: (one)-two-one-one and (one)-one-two-one. The "(one)" always symbolizes the goalie.

For the coach, three-zone drills offer the possibilities of improving the technique, tactical skills, and physical condition of a team. These exercises are useful for all ages, and offer a great number of variations:

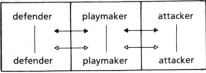

- Each player remains in his own zone.
- The player who passes the ball to the combination in the next zone enters that zone and creates a situation of numerical superiority.
- The combinations can be free, playing first-time kicks, or playing after a minimum number of touches.
- One or more shooters can be outside the touchlines and goal lines of the playing area.
- You can use a wild card (neutral player with different jersey from the two teams) to play on whichever team has the ball—only one for the three playing areas, one for the middle playing area, or one for each.

The objectives of this exercise vary. The coach can convey a certain objective or can just observe and analyze to detect general mistakes and try to correct them.

In this type of training, playing is more important than just doing drills. This will increase the fun of the game and improve performance.

### Objectives of the Exercise

- Learning to function in each playing zone, attacking, making the play, and defending
- Improving the one-on-one situation through the offense (by obtaining numerical superiority)
- Taking position just at the right moment to receive a pass from the other playing area
- Protecting the ball by dribbling so that you can pass at the right time
- Achieving high execution speed with direct playing

The backup player calls for the ball from behind (photos 1 through 6). One player (with the ball in his hand) will make the free shot. Two others are on each side, and the fourth player is on the far right side. When he puts the ball on the ground, the first player passes to the fourth one, who is running while the other two cross. The third player passes behind the first one and in front of the second one. The ball reaches the fourth player, who makes a direct pass to the third player, who comes from outside and tries to score.

The backup player in front calls for the ball (photos 7 through 14). The second series of photos shows practically the same execution, although the second and third players request the ball in front, and the fourth passes to the second, who shoots. This exercise requires lots of practice to achieve a smooth execution. Concentration, timing, and ball control are essential.

Naturally, many more possibilities exist, and you should leave room for other solutions. The other team's defense may be prepared for this specific play.

1

2

3

4

5

6

7

8

9

10

11

12

13

14

- Turning the advantage of numerical superiority (two-on-one) into goals
- Learning to overcome the difficulty of numerical inferiority (one-on-two)
- Learning to improve the one-two combination by using shooters who are outside the playing area
- Learning to improve the side playing in the system (one)-two-on-one

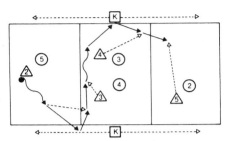

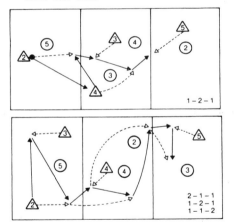

1-2-1

2-1-1
1-2-1
1-1-2

The player who passes to the other playing area also changes playing areas.

With two shooters on the touchlines:

With a wild card who can play in each half of the playing area and who always causes a situation of superiority (but who cannot shoot):

With three wild cards (one per zone) who must stay in their own zone, always playing with the team which has the ball but without passing among themselves or shooting:

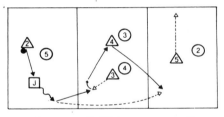

The possibilities are endless. A good, creative coach will make his choice and discover new forms through variations or by imposing limitations such as touching the ball as few times as possible or only once. One thing must always be clear: this exercise is only a means and never an end in itself. The objective of this exercise is to learn to play better indoor soccer.

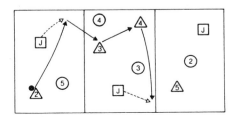

## Advantages of the Game

Free kicks, starting kickoffs, throw-ins, and corner kicks produce an advantage. They are a way of penalizing the team that made the infraction, and they offer the other team an advantage. To make use of the advantage, players could discuss the new situation, but, in fact, teams have only a minimum amount of time for penalty shots and no time for discussion. Here are two examples of how to proceed with the game (see pages 94 through 97).

### Initial kickoff
- Direct pass
- Take position
- Beat opponent
- Score early goal
- Prepare for opponent to approach
- Organize

Kickoffs look so simple! Two players are at the center line not too far from each other. The advance player makes the ball move. (The game starts after the ball makes one complete rotation.) Normally the ball goes to the second player, close to the center of the field, and then the players organize a certain play. They often play to their own side of the field, and sometimes they dribble or pass to a third player instead.

We want to point out some possibilities of kicking off, keeping in mind that a coach can dream up many more.

When making a direct pass at the maximum speed of the ball to one or two players who have taken up good position, you can beat the opposing team by obtaining an early goal and upsetting them:

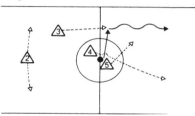

- Player 5, the advance player, shoots.
- Player 4, in the center, jumps over the ball.
- Player 3, on the left side, requests the ball and then dribbles towards the goal line.
- Player 4 makes a deep pass on the right side.
- Player 5 runs ahead through the center.
- Player 2 backs him up.

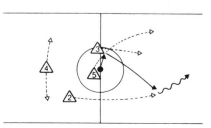

- Player 5 passes to Player 3, on the left side, and takes up position on the left side.
- Player 3 makes a direct pass to Player 2, on the right side, who looks for a position and advances through the center.
- Player 2 dribbles towards the goal line.
- Player 4 backs him up.

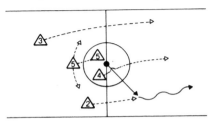

- Player 5 passes to Player 2, on the right, who takes position and leans slightly backwards to protect his back.
- Player 4 jumps over the ball and advances through the center.
- Player 3, on the left side, takes position on the left side.
- Player 2, on the right side, dribbles towards the goal line.

### Observations

In almost all the cases, the team has numerical superiority. Three of the four players run towards the opposite side of the playing area and look for the touchlines and goal lines. They should play the ball directly and at the maximum speed possible.

(Technical ability is important here!) This could create three-on-two situations, because the opponent feels beaten and becomes disorganized. Scoring is important. If the attack finds strong resistance or a turnover occurs because of a bad pass, the defense must set up quickly. The training of the backup players is important, including the assigned tasks of each player: man-to-man defense, zone defense, etc. Obviously, all this depends on the technical and tactical abilities of the players, as long as the level of the opponents is similar. In other words, the kickoff can offer great advantages and prevent the traditional backfield playing.

### Initial kickoff

- Direct pass
- Take position
- Stay away
- Maintain possession of the ball
- Organize

The game starts with a kickoff, kicking the ball from the center of the field towards the opponent's side. The players will be on their own side of the playing area, and the opponents must be out of the center circle.

The initial kickoff begins the match after halftime and starts play after a goal. (Rule VIII of the game. Initial kickoff.)

The first pass presents no great advantage because the opponent is only ten ft (3 m) from the ball, especially if the team places many of its players close to the ball.

Using only one player close to the kickoff to receive the ball, to first-time kick it, or to return it to the player who made the kickoff is better strategy.

Although we only offer two examples here, many more possibilities exist, and the coach should choose the best ones for his team.

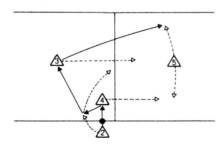

- Player 2, on the right side, kicks off to Player 4, in the center, receives the ball again, and passes it to Player 3, on the left side (one-two combination or give-and-go).
- Player 3 plays directly towards Player 5, the advance player, who is moving through the center and taking up position.
- Player 4 takes up position on

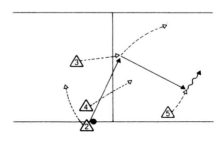

the right side and Player 2 backs him up.
- Player 2 passes to Player 3, and Player 4 jumps over the ball.
- Player 3 passes to Player 5, who takes up position towards the goal line.
- Player 4 advances through the center, and Player 2 backs him up.
- Player 3 is available on the left side.

*Corner Throw-in*
- Make direct pass
- Take position
- Use one of the players on the sides
- Take possession of the ball
- Organize

When a defensive player is the last to touch a ball that crosses the goal line without scoring, a player from the attacking team has five seconds to make a corner throw-in, using both hands and passing the ball over his

93

head. His feet must be on the ground outside the field, and he must be looking at the field from the corner angle formed by the touchline and the goal line (Rule XII of the game. Corner throw-in).

Here's one play for a course, that players don't have much time (only five seconds) to prepare:

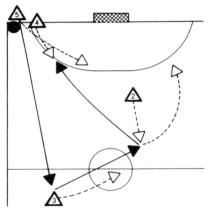

- Player 5, the advance player, does the corner throw-in and passes to Player 3, on the left side.
- Player 3 passes to Player 2, on the right side.
- Player 2 passes directly to Player 4, in the center, who has been away from the play.
- Player 5 takes position in front of the goal, and Player 3 backs him up.
- Now Player 2 takes position on the right side.

## Speed, Pressure, and Physical Condition

Indoor soccer players must be proficient in both attack and defense. A team must attack when it has the ball and defend when it loses the ball, working hard to recover it.

This requires:
- Great technical ability
- A good sense of the game
- Ability to pressure the opponent
- Optimal physical condition

Indoor soccer also has to be attractive as a spectacle for the fans. Speed is the main ingredient for this. Speed refers to both the speed of the ball and to the players on attack. Preferably, the players should run lengthwise along the playing area. They should also be able to maintain a slow and variable pace when needed. This slow pace requires them to keep possession of the ball. By changing pace, the players avoid risks. With fast execution the attacking team can break the defense, finding gaps that allow the team to score. At the same time, they are pressing the opponent. This is why great physical condition is necessary.

In general, the pace of the game is based on:
- The speed of the ball and the

momentum of play
- The speed with which the players handle the ball
- Timing and the speed at which the players take up position
- Teamwork

Another advantage of fast play is that the opponents can hardly take part in the game. In the case of a turnover, the opponents frequently lose the ball quickly. Pressing means attacking from the first minute of play. The objective is trying to beat the opponents so that they make mistakes and you can score.

Maintaining a quick pace playing and pressing the opponent requires great physical conditioning. Conditioning should start before the beginning of the season training so that the team can be in good shape technically, tactically, physically, and psychologically.

Good training always follows clear and logical thinking with a balanced relationship between play and rest, enough learning opportunities, and proper attention to important physical needs.

Such concepts as duration, intensity, and number of repetitions are fundamental. By duration, we mean the amount of time that players practice a spe-cific drill. Intensity is the level of energy used, at high speed or at a certain pace, with or without defense, individual (one-on-one) or with more players, with or without finishing with a goal. The number of repetitions refers to the number of times the players perform the drill.

We can incorporate all of this into an assortment of empirical "formulas":
- long duration + low intensity = most repetitions
- short duration + high intensity = many repetitions
- long duration + high intensity = no repetitions
- short duration + low intensity = many repetitions

Because of the way his players behave and the way they execute a drill, an experienced coach will quickly notice if they need a break. Players may lose concentration because they are tired, because they have repeated the drill too many times, or because the drill is too difficult. At this point, the players should have an active or passive break. Active ones could involve juggling the ball, walking, or even listening to the coach's instructions.

If the coach is also in charge of the physical conditioning, he will be able to use this training for plays and matches in order to synchronize the team and help it find its own style of playing. This will be good for both the regular players and for the many substitute players used in indoor soccer. A team of five regular players must have seven substitute ones. The coach can change players anytime during the match, and a player who comes out can go back in later on. The coach can make changes for technical reasons, such as for a player who is not performing at his best, or for physical reasons. Playing at high speed has an effect on a player's physical condition.

## Analysis of the Match

Analysis divides the game in parts in order to comprehend the whole. It consists of understanding what happened. The coach analyzes the game or the players by looking carefully.

Analyzing a match may involve making a report on a player, on a team, or on a potential opponent, based on technical ability, physical shape, system of play and speed of execution.

An analysis can be useful in helping to improve and/or adjust the style of play of an entire team or of each individual player to reach a certain objec-

tive in practices or to prepare for future opponents.

The starting point in observing and analyzing is the personal vision of the observer, including his expections and whether or not the players meet them. Because of the possibility of preconceived ideas which may not always be objective, a coach should also use other means, such as videos, questionnaires, or independent observers to provide an objective analysis.

Although videos are an excellent way to analyze high-level competition, in many indoor soccer matches questionnaires may be good enough. In order to design a well-structured questionnaire, you need to ask the following questions:

- What is your personal view of indoor soccer?
- Which initial premises are important in indoor soccer?
- How far can this team go?
- How can they achieve this objective?

When the view is the sum of knowledge, ability, and position, the coach should compare the view with the starting points, objectives, and the way to achieve them.

### Analysis of the Match
- Match: Score
- Break

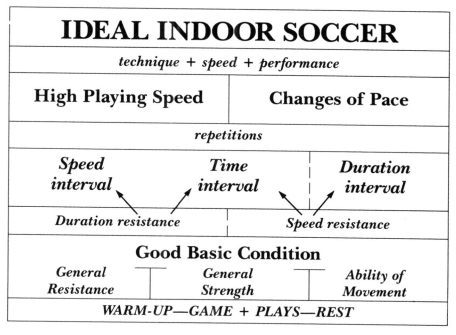

# IDEAL INDOOR SOCCER

*technique + speed + performance*

| **High Playing Speed** | **Changes of Pace** |
|---|---|

*repetitions*

| *Speed interval* | *Time interval* | *Duration interval* |
|---|---|---|
| *Duration resistance* | | *Speed resistance* |

## Good Basic Condition

| *General Resistance* | *General Strength* | *Ability of Movement* |
|---|---|---|

*WARM-UP—GAME + PLAYS—REST*

- Type of competition: exhibition, promotional, tournament, etc.

**Home team**
Number: Name
1
2
3
4
5
6
7
8
9
10

**Guest team**
Number: Name
1
2
3
4
5
6
7
8
9
10

Peculiarities.

Short description of the first half of the match.

Short description of the second half of the match.

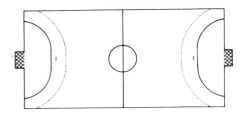

### Defense

- Evaluate the transition from attack to defense.
- Evaluate the system of defense.
- Evaluate the backup.
- Evaluate the team rapport.
- Where and how does the defense start (blocking, returning to own side, stopping the opponent)?
- Does the team defend correctly and at the right time? Do they start one-on-one plays?

### Attack

- Does the goalie take part in the game? How?
- Are there any limitations or conditions to the game?
- Evaluate the rapport and help from each player.
- How do the players move without the ball? Do they create spaces?
- Is there a counterattack? Evaluate.
- What is the main system?
- Evaluate the transition from defense to attack.

- Does the structure of the attack always follow the same guidelines?
- How do plays end?
- How does the team/player continue the play?

When analyzing all of these qualities (both positive and negative) in a certain player, you must consider the following aspects:

### Physical

Speed (starting and running), flexibility, and endurance

### Technical

Dribbling, receiving, passing, shooting, completing, solving the one-on-ones (speed, how strong the opponents were, does the team play in a space that is too large or too small)

### Tactical

- When in possession of the ball: timing, passing precision, getting open, approaching the ball, creating spaces
- After losing the ball: backing up the play, following the location of the ball, recovering the ball at the right moment and in the right way

### Psychological

Personality, behavior with the other players and the referee, ability and willingness to take advice, self-confidence, attitude towards competition

Because indoor soccer requires constant high speed, the coach will want to evaluate his players individually.

### Individual Player Report

The value of an individual report for each player is that you can write down all the information about a player and use it even during the match (during the halftime or moments when he is not playing) to help him correct weaknesses in his game. In this way, the player obtains a better view of his performance based on precise information. The objective of this report is to stimulate performance. In observing, analyzing, and reporting, the coach must be very objective and that is where the participation of several people can help guarantee an objective report.

| Match | Score | Halftime |
|-------|-------|----------|
| Type of match: (exhibition, promotional, tournament) | | |
| Peculiarities of match or arena: | | |
| Player's name: | Date of Birth: | |
| Player's address: | | |
| Team's name: | Category: | |
| Team's secretary: | | |

Is the speed of the game:
- low and negative
- average
- variable
- high and beneficial

1. Is this specific player more of an attack, defense, or balanced player?
2. What is his technical ability?
3. What is his attitude?
4. Evaluate his body control.
5. Evaluate his ability to move.
6. What is his physical shape?
7. What is his personality as a player?
8. How does he play in a team?
9. What are his qualities as a leader?
10. What is his body structure?
11. Does he play with his left, right, or both legs?
12. What is his average speed of play (slow, medium, variable, high)?
13. What is his position on the team?
14. Evaluate his ability to score.
15. How does he resolve one-on-ones?
16. Does he make many mistakes?
17. What is his behavior with referees and linesmen?
18. Does he accept direction?
19. List other specific observations.

Apart from this report for each player, which the coach can fill out after the match, he and his assistants can take other notes during the game. To complete the report, the coach can fill out this simple form.

March . . . . . . . . . . . . . . . . . . . .  Halftime score . . . . . . . . . .  Final score . . . . . . . . .

Date . . . . . . . . . . . . . . . . . . . .  Time . . . . . . . . . . . . . .

Coach . . . . . . . . . . . . . . . . .  Special conditions . . . . . . . . . .

| n⁰ Number Player's name | Turnovers | Recoveries | Assists | Possibilities of goal | Goals | Infractions (minutes) | First half | | | | | | Second half | | | | | Observations opposing team |
|---|---|---|---|---|---|---|---|---|---|---|---|---|---|---|---|---|---|---|
| | | | | | | | 1 | 2 | 3 | 4 | 5 | | 1 | 2 | 3 | 4 | 5 | |
| K K | | | | | | | 1 | | | | | 1 | | | | | | |
| 2 | | | | | | | 2 | | | | | 2 | | | | | | |
| | | | | | | | 3 | | | | | 3 | | | | | | |
| 3 | | | | | | | 4 | | | | | 4 | | | | | | |
| | | | | | | | 5 | | | | | 5 | | | | | | |
| 4 | | | | | | | 6 | | | | | 6 | | | | | | |
| | | | | | | | 7 | | | | | 7 | | | | | | |
| 5 | | | | | | | 8 | | | | | 8 | | | | | | |
| | | | | | | | 9 | | | | | 9 | | | | | | |
| 6 | | | | | | | 10 | | | | | 10 | | | | | | |
| | | | | | | | 11 | | | | | 11 | | | | | | |
| 7 | | | | | | | 12 | | | | | 12 | | | | | | |
| | | | | | | | 13 | | | | | 13 | | | | | | |
| 8 | | | | | | | 14 | | | | | 14 | | | | | | |
| | | | | | | | 15 | | | | | 15 | | | | | | |
| 9 | | | | | | | 16 | | | | | 16 | | | | | | Observations this team |
| | | | | | | | 17 | | | | | 17 | | | | | | |
| | | | | | | | 18 | | | | | 18 | | | | | | |
| | | | | | | | 19 | | | | | 19 | | | | | | |
| | | | | | | | 20 | | | | | 20 | | | | | | |
| | | | | | | | 21 | | | | | 21 | | | | | | |
| | | | | | | | 22 | | | | | 22 | | | | | | |
| | | | | | | | 23 | | | | | 23 | | | | | | |
| TOTAL: | | | | | | | 24 | | | | | 24 | | | | | | |
| | | | | | | | 25 | | | | | 25 | | | | | | |

Here's another example of a similar form. Keep in mind that each coach can create his own form.

# Individual Player's Report

Name: ...........................  Address: ..........................  Observations:

Date of birth: .....................  ..........................

Team: ...........................  Match: ..........................

Position on team: ..................  Halftime score: ....................

Date: ...........................  Final score: ......................

| Time playing | Good pass /Good action | Assists | Goals | Goal chances | Recovered balls | Poor pass/ action | Infractions | Observations |
|---|---|---|---|---|---|---|---|---|
| 1. |  |  |  |  |  |  |  | Technical qualities |
| 2. |  |  |  |  |  |  |  |  |
| 3. |  |  |  |  |  |  |  |  |
| 4. |  |  |  |  |  |  |  |  |
| 5. |  |  |  |  |  |  |  |  |
| 6. |  |  |  |  |  |  |  | Tactical qualities |
| 7. |  |  |  |  |  |  |  |  |
| 8. |  |  |  |  |  |  |  |  |
| 9. |  |  |  |  |  |  |  |  |
| 10. |  |  |  |  |  |  |  |  |
| 11. |  |  |  |  |  |  |  |  |
| 12. |  |  |  |  |  |  |  | Physical character- istics |
| 13. |  |  |  |  |  |  |  |  |
| 14. |  |  |  |  |  |  |  |  |
| 15. |  |  |  |  |  |  |  |  |
| 16. |  |  |  |  |  |  |  |  |
| 17. |  |  |  |  |  |  |  |  |
| 18. |  |  |  |  |  |  |  |  |
| 19. |  |  |  |  |  |  |  | Psycholog- ical qualities |
| 20. |  |  |  |  |  |  |  |  |
| 21. |  |  |  |  |  |  |  |  |
| 22. |  |  |  |  |  |  |  |  |
| 23. |  |  |  |  |  |  |  |  |
| 24. |  |  |  |  |  |  |  |  |
| 25. |  |  |  |  |  |  |  |  |
|  | GP = good pass GA = good action | A = assists | A = goal with assistance I = individual goal | GA = goal attempts | I = intermed- iate | PP = poor pass PA = poor action | PC = personal contact 3 = 3 min. |  |

# Coaches and the Importance of Observing

Substituting players is very normal in indoor soccer. Replaced players come back to the game later. Coaches substitute for tactical reasons or because of a player's physical condition.

Substituting players should not be a problem in indoor soccer but, in fact, teams don't often practice these changes, and the dialogue between the team and the coach does not normally take place until moments before the match begins. By then, little time is left, not enough room is available, and sometimes the locker room is too hot. Not an ideal situation. The team wants to get out of the locker room as soon as possible.

By definition, training is supposed to positively affect behavior. In indoor soccer, this means influencing the behavior of the players to make them play according to a previously determined strategy or style of play. That is the job of a coach.

The ideal coach's personality includes these characteristics:

- emotional stability, even under strong psychological pressure
- good organizational skills
- openness and confidence in the team
- leadership
- self-criticism
- ability to speak in a direct way
- technical knowledge
- winning mentality
- public relations skills with the fans and the press

Being a coach requires great technical knowledge and good rapport with the team. The coach must know the specific techniques and concepts of playing the sport and know how to communicate them to the players. Study and experience are essential. Taking courses, chatting with other coaches and watching demonstrations, observing, and analyzing other coaches are all important. Finally, each coach must develop his own style, determined by his own personality.

Because of his great technical knowledge, a coach usually doesn't easily change his mind about a particular system or

The coach must have technical knowledge of the sport. He must be experienced himself and must understand the concepts of playing it. Above all, he must know how to communicate these ideas to the players. This requires study and experience. Each coach will develop his own style, depending on his personality. This style can cause humorous reactions from the players, like the ones in the photo from a Dutch indoor soccer team.

style. If he does, he may unconsciously transmit his own fear to the players. The players will not understand his worries, and the tension will increase.

Certain players, and especially those who have the most influence on the style of play, dominate the style and can cause chaos unless the coach establishes the style of play. The coach forms the team based on the available players. The objective is to achieve a final result which depends on the strength of the team as a whole.

The goalie's main task is to stop the ball, and when he does it correctly, he will show other qualities:
- ability to defend the outside, throwing the ball and/or building the play
- ending with a kick to the op-

ponent's goal from the center field
- guiding, giving pointers, setting the pace

Forcing a goalie who does not take part in the game to start plays is usually disappointing and has a negative effect on the team's playing form.

Forcing the players to play in a way that they cannot perform is frustrating. This is true for the side players as well as for the center and advance players.

A good coach observes and analyzes the playing behavior of his team and gives his opinion to all the players. A team in which each player knows about the technical, tactical, and physical qualities of the others will make good use of that information both when they have the ball and after they have lost it, whether they are winning or losing. The coach can help with simple and calm instructions during the match.

We have no perfect "recipe" for an ideal team, a team that always wins. To create a successful team, either with young talent or with experienced players from other teams, the players must have a mutual understanding. They must get along and complement one another.

An advance player depends

on one or both side players or the approaching center player—not too early, not too late, but at the right moment. In indoor soccer, we are talking about fractions of a second.

An advance player can be good in the individual game or in completing the plays after receiving the ball from the wings—controlling, passing or, even better, passing without controlling. He can shoot if he has an opportunity, eliminate a defender, or clear the way for himself or for the center player.

An advance player can be mobile, but he can also be static without losing his function. In terms of defense, his role can be only fair because he is not having a good day or because he is completely overwhelmed by his opponent.

Because of the great psychical pressure associated with the position, the advance player can get into trouble with the rules of the game—and with the coach.

The coach must know how to observe all of this.

Observing is the union of what the coach sees and theory. Theory is all of the knowledge, experience, and sports history of the coach.

To use theory, a coach must be able to reason properly and to give solid arguments. This involves much more than just having an idea of what dribbling is, how to make a good pass, or what a good defense is. Elements of seeing, hearing, and intuition are part of observation. The observation is a function of only one person, the coach.

The only way of finding out if someone else shares your observation is to compare ideas, to talk about it without preconceived notions of what is correct.

However, a coach cannot always compare or talk about what he sees. Often he must act quickly and decisively.

Talking about taking action and correcting players and systems raises the following question: What do you do with what you have observed?

A good coach will be objective with his players at the beginning of the match. He will not have a negative attitude towards any of them. He must know the qualities of all the players and their limitations. When the match begins, he has to concentrate on:
• the progress of the match
• team rapport
• opponents
• individual games
• the form of play
• players' physical condition

Obviously, a coach cannot observe all of this. He must anticipate what he should do before the match begins and after he receives the last report. During the match, he must be able to make the necessary changes using the following to guide him:
1. What am I going to see?
2. What do I want to see?
3. What do I see?
4. What do I do with it?
5. What else must I see?
6. How is the system of play working?
7. Which player is not performing?
8. Which players must be changed?
9. Could another player be the solution?
10 What instructions should I give?

A coach with prejudices cannot make objective observations. His theoretical arguments will lean towards the emotional rather than towards the theoretical. The coach must guide the behavior of others, a nice but difficult task.

Theory determines what has to be observed and why. If the observation coincides with the theory, then the observation will not require the coach's intervention. The coach should not rush to judgment simply because his team is behind at the moment. An observant coach always attempts to collect all possible information to reach a balanced understanding that will allow each player and the entire team to solve problems.

## Training in Indoor Soccer

| | |
|---|---|
| During practice matches ........................ | 10 percent |
| During the game/in halftime ................... | 70 percent |
| Through conversations with the team ........... | 20 percent |

In indoor soccer, training during the game is most important. Even if the game has no timeouts, the coach can influence the development of the game by changing players, which can increase the pace of the game or change the style of playing by increasing or decreasing the number of attackers.

Often the coach's intervention involves yelling, which can be uncomfortable for the fans and referee. The rules of the game do not allow coaches to come onto the playing area because a coach can make his team function properly with a minimum amount of screaming.

This is why we advise using silent practice sessions with hand and arm signals to give instructions to the team. Each coach can make up a series of signals and gestures that only his team knows. They can be for the whole team or just for the leader.

1. The left hand and the forearm are in front of the body, parallel to the touchline. The right arm makes a pushing movement towards the other half of the playing area. (If the team is playing in the other half, invert the arm movements.) PLAY ALONG THE LENGTH AND WIDTH OF THE PLAYING AREA.

2. The right (or left) hand makes a fist and hides it behind the left (or right) hand. The coach bends slightly forward. COVER TIGHTLY.

3. The left and right forearm rotate. MOVE THE BALL MORE EFFECTIVELY.

4. Both hands are raised just above the touchline. MAINTAIN POSSESSION OF THE BALL WITH FIRST-TIME PASSES.

These are only examples intended to help coaches create their own signals. They should be creative for the benefit of the game and the players.

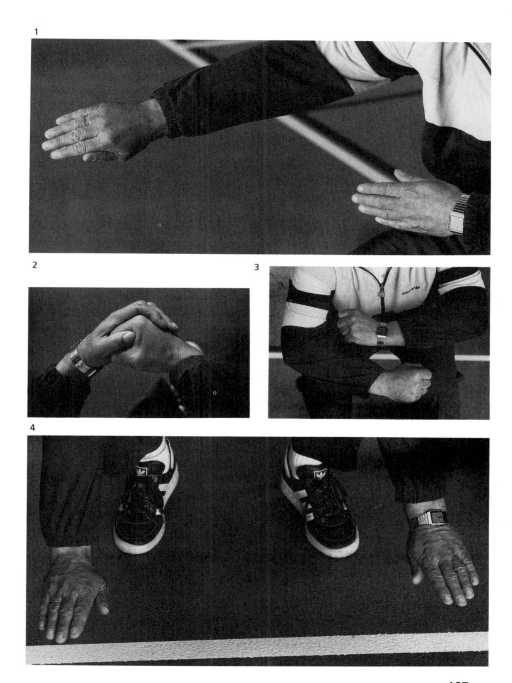

# Circuit Training to Improve Technical Skills

Circuit training is very appropriate for indoor soccer, especially if the diverse stages require technical ability:

- Players can improve technical ability and become more automatic with the repetitions in each stage.
- A greater number of players can practice at the same time with fixed and limited drills.
- This type of training requires a relatively small space.
- The players improve their physical condition when you combine this with other training exercises.
- The speed increases quickly as opposed to the increase in muscle resistance.
- Circuit training presents no organizational problems for the coach.

Obviously, indoor circuit training can be inconvenient. Due to the high temperature, players will perspire more freely, giving the impression that they are training very hard. This can have a negative effect on their motivation to work harder or to stay motivated during the entire practice session.

The aim of circuit training is to increase ball control in a high-speed game. Due to the limitations of working with the ball (depending on the technical aptitude), the intensity will vary, and the training will not be optimal during the entire time.

If we divide the circuit training into: (1) individual practice; (2) practice with a teammate (kicking or throwing to him); (3) group practice in taking turns; (4) all pairs practicing at the same time; then circuit training and working in pairs that are practicing at the same time works well.

When working at the same time as the rest of the team, the results will depend on good cooperation. This is why it is helpful to pair players with similar technical qualities and physical build. The similarities will lead to better execution, fewer bad passes, and consistent ball speed.

COACHES AND THE IMPORTANCE OF OBSERVING

However, the training routines should not be too difficult.

A coach does better using five or six good exercises and one round (repetition) than when he tries to maintain the same performance for each exercise:

- The players have to achieve optimal concentration.
- They have to correctly execute the technique.
- The coach has to choose a known technique.

We have already mentioned that the coach must choose easy circuits, with exercises known by all players. He will have to briefly explain to the players what each exercise is for so that they can obtain some experience, know the objective, and not lose valuable time during practice sessions. Use exercises in the warm-up. The team can achieve the knowledge and experience of the execution and the objective during the warm-up phase. Stretching exercises and some time to relax can be the last part of the warm-up and the beginning of the circuit training. In this way, the coach will have the chance to change or reduce an exercise that does not work or that seems too difficult.

The coach can make the circuit harder or easier by:

- making the distances between cones and return marks larger
- shortening break time
- increasing the number of repetitions
- increasing intensity and reducing break time and vice versa (always in an irregular way)

Because of the limited possibilities of training in indoor soccer (the ratio of match to training is around four to one), we have intentionally chosen circuit training with exercises that need a teammate, since apart from obtaining and maintaining basic physical conditioning shape, the players must achieve skill in controlling the ball.

The coach should determine which exercises are important and then decide the level of the training.

### Stage 1

Start, dribble, receive the ball at medium height. Two cones 25 feet (8 m) apart and two balls.

At the same time, each player kicks his ball slightly to the left or right, towards the other player. The players have to run quickly towards the ball, receive it with a half turn, control it, take it in one movement, and then dribble back to the starting cone. They repeat the exercise immediately.

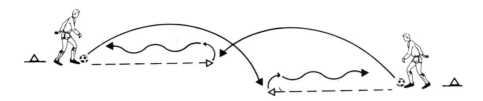

## Stage 2

Start, sprint, dribble, relay. Two cones 30 feet (10 m) apart and one ball.

Player A dribbles from his cone towards Player B, who is approaching slowly. Player B takes the ball and dribbles around Player A's cone. After having passed the ball, Player A runs towards Player B's cone and returns slowly towards Player B, who is dribbling.

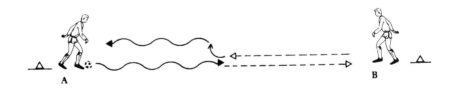

## Stage 3

Dribbling, passing, receiving the ball with a half turn. Two cones 25 feet (8 m) apart and two balls.

Both players dribble towards the other, pass the ball, receive it with a half turn, and dribble around their own cones. After this, they repeat the exercise.

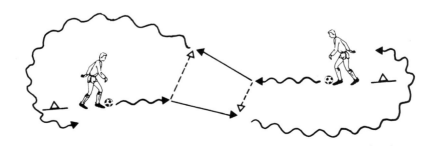

## Stage 4

Passing, turning, sprinting. Two cones 30 feet (10 m) apart and one ball.

Player A passes the ball fast to Player B, turns, and runs around his own cone. Then he receives the ball. Player B also turns quickly and runs around his cone. The players must use the foot closest to the ball and use both the inside and outside of the foot. They may turn to the left or to the right after playing the ball.

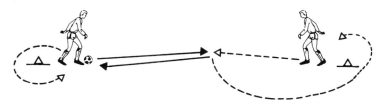

## Stage 5

Dribbling, receiving the ball, cutting, and turning. Two cones 25 feet (8 m) apart and two balls.

Both players dribble towards each other and meet almost at the center. Each stops his ball under his foot and runs towards the other's ball. Then, they continue dribbling. At the left or right of the cone, the players cut the ball with the inside or outside of the foot. After this, they dribble, and, near the center, they stop the ball under their feet.

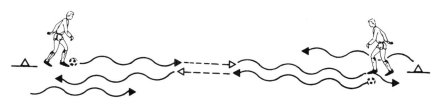

## Stage 6

Passing the ball, starting, running, and sprinting. Four cones 12 to 25 feet (4 to 8 m) apart and two balls.

Both players pass the ball with the same speed and direction at the same time on the larger side of the right corner area. After a quarter turn towards their starting position, they run and pass again with the inside or outside of the feet, watching their teammate. The coach can help by adjusting the speed of the ball.

These are only six examples. A coach can create many more using one, two, three, or four cones, benches leaning on their sides, and the walls of the room.

After players complete the circuit several times with the same exercises, dribbling, passing, and receiving the ball will become automatic. The speed of the ball will increase, as will the precision. In other words, the series of actions will increase, and the circuit becomes a test of technical skills which will motivate and stimulate the players.

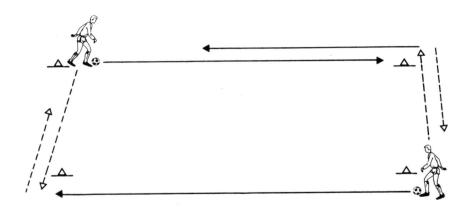

# Preparation

## Warm-Up

The lack of a warm-up period or a bad warm-up can cause injuries. Warm-ups are really very important.

Some of the arguments in support of a short warm-up are "That's enough," "I want action," "I'm already in shape," "Let me work with the ball," and "I got here by bicycle." The objective of the warm-up is to increase performance through physical and psychological conditioning. The warm-up is intended to:

- increase the temperature of the muscles
- improve the blood flow in the muscles
- stimulate digestion
- adjust the blood circulation, the heart, and the respiratory system
- make muscles, tendons, and ligaments more flexible
- reduce the risk of injuries
- improve the coordination between nerves and muscles
- increase the motivation to compete (training)
- help a player get into the game and perform
- help him forget everything but the game

In addition to warming up the muscles, players can also "elongate" them with stretching exercises, preferably after the first warm-up exercises and before finishing. For example:

The players should arrive half an hour early. The locker rooms are warm, and their muscles will not get cold. After changing, they can start the warm-up with some stretching exercises, sitting on the bench, standing against the wall, etc. They can do all back, thigh, leg, and foot muscle stretches.

Warm-ups eliminate muscle tension to achieve more elasticity in the joints and improve blood flow. They also produce psychological advantages. For example, the players become calmer and start the game more relaxed. In most cases, only five to ten minutes remain before the start of the game.

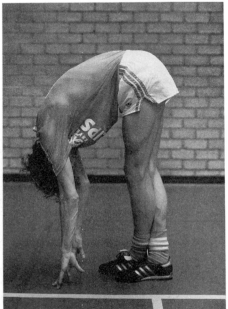

The team can enter the playing area and warm up with or without the ball, preferably lengthwise to the playing area to get the feel of playing in that direction. We also advise practicing diagonally and along the width of the field. Try changing the pace and including turns and directional changes, as well as little jumps and sprints. All of these exercises will put emphasis on leg movement. Finish up by doing some of the stretching exercises mentioned before (the ones that players do in the locker room).

Next, players should spend a few minutes handling the ball to warm up and get the feel of playing a match. Use one or two plays to conclude the warm-up. These can be the bridge to the start of the match or to introduce technical and tactical exercises in practice sessions.

### Example
After the players enter the playing area, they should start running along its length, slowly at first, and then increasing and decreasing the pace.

As we mentioned before, the players can then start a series of exercises to loosen up, such as several minutes of stretching followed by sprints and runs.

The player in the photos shows how you can eliminate excessive muscle tension and improve the elasticity in the joints and blood flow in the muscles through stretching exercises. Stretching the muscles prevents many injuries and is a good bridge from a break to an active period, from resting muscles to awakened muscles. When cats wake up, they first stretch, then they start their activity.

Then comes ball handling and several plays. After this, they can work in a reduced space, such as half of the playing area or a space defined with cones. If they use one small space, something like "catch and touch" can create more interest in the game and develop agility. If they use two defined spaces, we are unconsciously promoting a "winning mentality."

The exercise requires two similar spaces, two types of jerseys, two to five players.

The players cannot leave their own area. Both teams appoint a "catcher." The goal is to catch as many players of the other team as possible in a certain amount of time (for example, thirty, forty-five, or sixty seconds). Whoever touches the most

players on the other team wins one point. If there is a tie, one gets a point. Next, they try with one ball in each area with the same formation. The players throw the ball in their own area with their hands. The ball cannot touch the floor, and they cannot walk or run with it. The "catcher" tries to touch the player who has the ball in his hands.

***Variations***

1. Relays with the ball.
2. The ball cannot be returned to the last player who had it.
3. Play the ball with the feet, with limited touches, and then with only one or two touches.

The catcher tries to touch the player who has the ball. He tries to steal the ball. If the ball goes

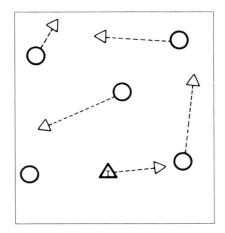

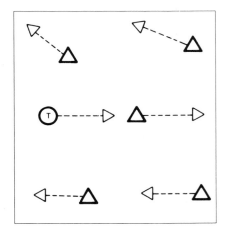

out of the area, it becomes an advantage situation for the catcher.

The third variation is only appropriate for technically skilled players.

### Observation

This form of play is perfect for a tactical exercise. The coach will instruct the players exactly what position to take. They have to use the spaces well, creating the possibility of a third and fourth pass, to achieve the most direct game possible. In this second part of the warm-up, five-on-five or six-on-six play is appropriate. The players are already wearing different jerseys.

### Plays

With the hands:
- throw
- catch

The team trying to steal the ball tries to:
- touch the player who has the ball
- touch the ball
- recover the ball

With the feet (for technically skilled players):
- free (limited contact with the ball)
- touch the ball no more than three times
- touch the ball no more than two times

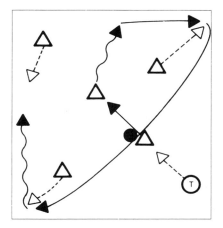

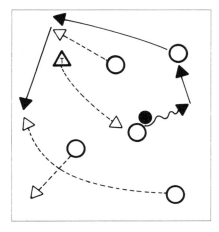

### Observation

The plays mentioned above are not simple. They require great technical ability (with both hands and feet) and great tactical maturity. This is why the coach should allow numerical superiority when players try this the first time. Team A (with the ball) should have five or six players and Team B only two or three. This is very close to a complete indoor soccer game of five-on-five (including goalies) with two goals. The coach can introduce some conditions here, such as trying to score from an individual game, from a pass, from a one-two combination, or from a relay.

## Bandaging and Immobilizing

An ounce of prevention is worth a pound of cure, as the saying goes. Preventive measures are fundamental. The team doctor or a physical therapist should treat any injuries. A sports medicine doctor should be the one to recommend treatment.

Indoor soccer games do not require the presence of a doctor, and a sports masseur or trainer may be more helpful. Few clubs give much thought to medical care. Even now, most players are not very well prepared to participate in competition. They don't spend time in practice sessions, and many are not in good physical shape.

In sports, especially in soccer, ankle injuries are the most frequent. The ankle is a complex and fragile joint.

The tibia and the fibula are the two bones which form the lower part of the leg. The end of the tibia forms the inside part of the ankle, and the end of the fibula forms the outside part. Together they make a bridge connecting the two big bones of the foot. Under normal circumstances, the ligaments of the ankle are strong enough to protect it from excessive lateral movement (twists). The back-and-forth movement is normal and necessary for leg movement, creating the foot movement from the heel to the toes (when walking or running).

Indoor soccer is very hard on the ankles. The playing surface is hard, and the feet cannot sink into the surface when running and turning. Weak ankles can easily twist in a forced lateral movement. This often involves the outside of the ankle. Swelling, sprains, twists, and even torn ligaments and tendons can be the result. Players need to take preventive measures.

We have already mentioned that this is the physical therapist's job, especially if a player needs protective bandages.

Fortunately, players can learn to apply their own preventive measures, following the basic rule that to protect the outside of the ankle from forced lateral movements, one stretches the bandage from the outside in.

Be sure the bandage can "breathe," is elastic, is coated with acrylic glue, is two to three inches (6–8 cm) wide, and is made of wool.

Apart from bandaging the ankle, you can also immobilize it in order to stabilize it in all directions. This should be left up to the physical therapist or to an expert in bandaging. A novice cannot immobilize an ankle without danger and should refrain from trying to do so.

## Indoor Soccer Shoes

Indoor soccer playing areas can vary considerably from slippery to rough. Players must adapt by controlling their bodies and by using the right kind of shoes.

Most injuries in this sport occur because of shoes which:
- have inadequate soles
- lack ankle support
- are the wrong size
- lack cushioning

An indoor soccer player with only one pair of shoes can have problems. Players should have a second pair with a different kind of sole. Most sports arenas do not accept shoes with black soles because the carbon in the rubber can mark the floor.

Although rubber is disappearing as a material for the soles of sport shoes, a white rub-

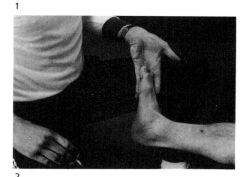

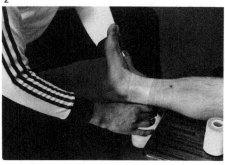

The physical therapist in the pictures shows some important steps in bandaging an ankle. First, be sure the bandage is clean, without any dirt from the ground or any moisture. Wrap gauze around the ankle to avoid skin and hair irritation and then wrap the bandage without wrinkling it. Include the heel and stretch the bandage slightly on every turn from the outside to the inside of the ankle to avoid twisting the outside part. Keep the pressure even as you wrap. Bandaging is a technique best left to a physical therapist or specialist. Immobilizing an ankle can be dangerous, and novices should refrain from doing it themselves.

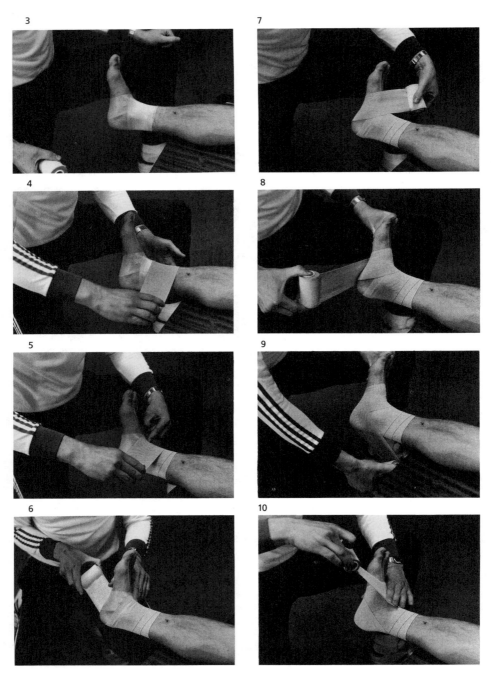

11

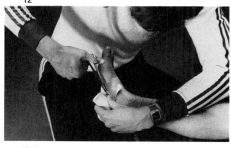

12

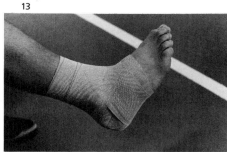

13

White rubber soles seem to be the most popular in this sport, and they do not mark the floor.

Natural rubber soles do not wear out so fast, but they are also rougher. Synthetic soles are strong and look good, but they are very sensitive to the surface temperature and dangerous if the floor is wet or moist.

Shoe soles are made from many different types of material and you can find even more variety in the surface pattern of the soles:

- flat and smooth
- fine ridges
- big ridges
- suction cups
- round, oval, or angular side ridges
- with or without turning area for the foot

Of course, this is partly a matter of personal preference, but the player must also consider the articulation of the ankle and his own physical makeup. Players need to be informed about these matters.

The tip of the foot must be free to have contact with the ball.

Normally, indoor soccer players prefer suede shoes because they are rough, which makes it easier to control the ball. Adding spin to the ball is a

ber sole can be just right. One with natural rubber will be even better. This is a natural product and is less responsive to temperature changes. The floors of the arenas (wood or artificial, permanent or removable flooring on concrete) can change considerably, depending on the temperature.

121

technical and functional weapon in this sport.

Suede is not very strong, and the shoe will not last very long.

Leather is not as rough, but it is stronger and has the same features as suede. It adapts very well to the shape of the feet. Ox leather is much stronger and rougher, although it offers less sensitivity to the ball. Kangaroo leather is similar to suede, relatively strong, but more expensive.

In indoor soccer, ankles, knees, and groin muscles are exposed to a great deal of pressure. Turning, running, and slowing down in a small area are typical in indoor soccer. Players use a lot of short and explosive movements, with or without the ball, in an area where there is less oxygen than in traditional soccer. Muscle fatigue can appear early on, increasing the risk of injury. A good coach must

Without a doubt, most injuries in indoor soccer are caused by wearing improper shoes. The type of sole is very important. Preferred soles are made of rubber with some support for turning on the ball of the foot. The soles should have reinforced heels and not be too thin to avoid twisting an ankle.

Players should have at least two kinds of shoes since the surface of the playing area can be anything from wood, linoleum, or concrete to artificial turf.

monitor the shoes of his players.

Indoor soccer requires strong shoes—"strong" meaning safe for the player, preventing injury, and making it easy to apply his technical skills:

- The sole needs to adapt well to the floor (rubber, reclaimed rubber, or synthetic).
- The shoe must provide good heel support to protect the ankles and, at the same time, allow for mobility in the game.
- The back edges cannot be too rounded to protect the ankles and avoid pressure.
- The shoes must have enough foot room, allowing for perspiration, and preferably be without nylon to avoid blisters.
- They must have a good tongue to avoid the pressure of the laces on the foot when hitting the ball.
- The soles cannot be too thin or the shoes won't have enough ankle support.
- They should be the proper size, not too wide to avoid blisters, but long enough to allow room for the feet to swell when they warm up.
- They must have well-tied shoe laces. If they are not properly tied, shoe laces can be a problem when kicking the ball.

# Rules of the Game

## Rule I. Playing Area

### 1. Dimensions

(a) The playing area should be 130 feet (40 m) by 65 feet (20 m). This area can be up to 6 feet (2 m) longer or shorter.

(b) A safety area should surround the edges of the playing area. In international competitions, this area must be at least 3 feet (1 m) from the touchlines and 6 feet (2 m) from the goal lines.

### 2. Defining the Playing Area

The lines should be 3 inches (8 cm) wide and marked as shown on page 143. The longest lines are the touchlines, and the short ones are the goal lines. The center runs the width of the playing area, dividing it into two equal halves. The center of the field has a clearly marked circle with a radius of 10 feet (3 m).

### 3. Penalty Area

The penalty area has three lines. The first is a straight line measuring 10 feet (3 m), which is parallel to the goal line and 20 feet (6 m) from it. The two other lines are two curves which result

from drawing two circles each with a radius of 20 feet (6 m). The center of each is the base of the goalposts. These lines connect the ends of the parallel line to the goal line.

### 4. Penalty Spot

Two circles with a radius of 4 inches (10 cm) are located 20 feet (6 m) from the center of each goal, measured from an imaginary line that would connect the centers of the goals. Players kick penalty shots from these spots.

### 5. Substitutions Area

(a) Along the touchline on which the players' benches sit are two lines 30 inches (78 cm) long. Fifteen inches (39 cm) are inside the playing area and 15 inches (39 cm) are outside. These lines extend 10 feet (3 m) along both sides of the center line. Players must use the area between these lines when they leave or enter the game during a substitution.

(b) The coaches will use the space from each of these lines to the end of the benches for time-outs.

## 6. Goals

(a) In the center of each goal line is a goal. It should be movable, not anchored to the ground, and have two vertical posts 10 feet (3 m) apart inside and connected at the top by a horizontal post placed 6 feet (2 m) from the ground (measured on the inside). The three posts must be 3 inches (8 cm) thick and all must be of equal width.

(b) Nets hang from the posts on the back of the goal, fixed on the back and bottom by curved tubes or some other adequate holding device.

(c)The three posts have alternating colors so that they stand out from the ground and the playing area. Generally, the colors are red and white. In the two angles formed by the vertical and horizontal posts, each paint stripe must be 11 inches (28 cm) long and of the same color. The rest of the stripes must each be 8 inches (20 cm).

## 7. Surface

The surface of the playing area—hardwood, rubber, wood, or linoleum—must be smooth and free of any rough areas.

## 8. Timekeeper's Table

Every playing area must have a central space inaccessible to the spectators with a table and chairs for the timekeeper and other officials. This should be at least 3 feet (1 m) from the touchline.

## 9. Substitute Players, Coaches, Doctors, and Team Assistants

These should be on the sides, a minimum of 10 feet (3 m) on each side of the timekeeper's table.

The home team chooses which bench it wants for the match.

No one on the bench may be closer than 10 feet (3 m) to the table. The coach is the only person who can talk to the timekeeper, and then only at authorized times.

## 10. Score Panels

The table referee should be perfectly visible to the players and the public. The area should have a score board and time clock to display the time remaining in the match and the score.

## 11. Height of the Arena

An indoor arena must have at least 15 feet (5 m) of unobstructed space above the floor.

## 12. Licensing

The organizing association for each competition must license arenas that do not meet the requirements described above.

## Rule II. Ball

1. The ball shall be one of the brands and models complying with established standards. The home team must furnish three balls which the referees will check.

2. The ball should have a circumference of between 23 and 24 inches (59–61 cm) and weigh between 14 and 15 ounces (410–430 gm).

3. When it is dropped 10 feet (2 m), the ball shall not bounce less than three times or more than four times.

4. Only a referee can approve a ball change during the match, although the team captains can ask to have a defective ball replaced. However, the referee makes the decision.

## Rule III. Number of Players

1. Each team has a maximum of five players, one of whom can play as a goalie.

The rules of each competition will determine the minimum number of players required on the field to start a match.

If for any reason a team has only three players during the game, the referee will stop the match.

2. The team can use substitute players in any match played by these rules.

3. The maximum number of players for a match is established as twelve.

4. The team can make as many substitutions as needed. A player who has come out of the game can return as a substitute. The referee needs to be informed of the intended changes.

5. The substitutions must follow these rules:

(a) The player being replaced must leave the field through the touchline in the change area.

(b) The substitute player must enter the field in the same area, but never before the other player is off the field.

(c) A substitute player must comply with the referee's authority, even if he does not play in that match.

(d) The change is complete when the substitute player enters the field, becoming a player.

(e) Substitutions take place during the game without stopping it, except when changing goalies.

6. The goalie can change positions with any other player as long as the referee knows about it. The clock stops for such substitutions.

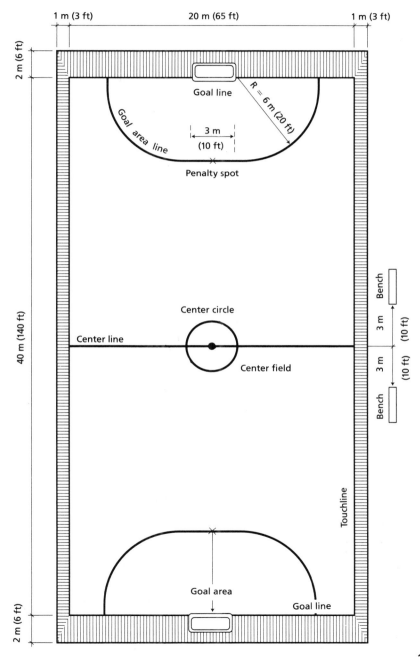

## Rule IV. Equipment

1. The players may not use any object considered dangerous by the referee.

2. The player's usual equipment includes a short-sleeve or long-sleeve jersey, short pants, socks, and shoes. Players must wear only canvas or soft leather shoes with soles made of rubber or other similar material. Players must wear shoes.

3. All players must have a number on their back. The numbers must be 6 inches (15 cm) to 8 inches (20 cm) high. The numbers must be between one and fifteen. The color of the number must be different from the color of the jersey. The number must also be on the front of the jersey or on the pants.

4. Only the goalie may wear long pants. He must wear different colors from the other players and from the referee.

5. A player not wearing the proper attire must leave the playing area until the referee authorizes his attire.

## Rule V. Referees

1. Each match will have two referees. Their authority as described in the RULES OF THE SPORT begins when they enter the arena where the match will take place and ends when they leave the arena.

2. During the match, they will call all the infractions, even during a temporary suspension of the game, and even when the ball is not in play. Their decisions are final.

3. They must comply with the following rules:

(a) They will apply all the rules.

(b) They will not impose a penalty that gives an advantage to the team that made the infraction.

(c) They will take notes of all incidents occurring before, during, and after the game.

(d) They will use their discretion when infractions occur. They may stop or suspend the match if they consider this necessary. In such cases, they will file a report with the appropriate association, within the time frame indicated by the rules.

(e) From the moment they arrive on the playing area, they can reprimand any player who displays an incorrect attitude. They can expel a player from the game if a foul recurs. In this case, they will report the name of the player to the appropriate association within the proper time frame in the manner determined by the rules.

(f) They shall not allow anyone other than the players to enter the playing area without their approval.

(g) They will interrupt the game to allow medical help in the case of a serious injury. In this case, the player must leave the playing area. He can return to the game later, when the ball is no longer moving. If medical assistance is not necessary, the game can continue without interruption. However, this rule does not apply to goalies.

(h) They shall disqualify any player from the game who, in their opinion, has displayed violence, rough play, or obscene behavior.

(i) They shall also disqualify, without warning, any player, trainer, coach, or any other person who displays poor morals or poor sportsmanship.

(j) When calling a foul, they will name the infraction. In the case of cumulative fouls, they will request that the table referee record them in the record of the match.

(k) They will give a signal to restart the game after any interruptions, except for goal kicks, throw-ins, and corner kicks.

(l) They will decide whether the ball meets the requirements described in Rule II.

# Rule VI. Table Referee

A table referee will be present for each match. He will be the timekeeper responsible for:

1. Recording the names of the players, the technical, personal, and cumulative fouls, the goals scored, the players who scored them, the warnings and expulsions, the time-outs, and anything related to the game at the referee's request.

2. Warning: using a whistle or other acoustic signal different than the referee's whistle at the end of the first and second halves. These signals, loud and relatively long, will cue the referees to start and end the match.

3. Notifying:

(a) The number and team of the player who commits the next-to-last cumulative foul.

(b) A player's fifth cumulative foul so the coach can replace him.

(c) The fifth team foul in each half so that the other team receives a free kick without a wall of players starting with the next foul.

4. Measuring the time with a chronometer:

(a) Starting the clock when the referee blows the whistle at the beginning of the match or in any other situation when the match has stopped.

(b) Stopping the clock when the referees so indicates during time-outs requested by the teams, when the ball goes out of bounds, and when the match stops. Starting the clock again when the ball begins to move.

(c) Not starting the clock until a kicking sequence in cases of a penalty or foul without a wall of players after the fifth cumulative foul per team. A kicking sequence is the intervention or participation of another player who touches the ball, unless the ball touches the goalie and goes into the goal. A kicking sequence also occurs when the ball touches the posts of the goal and does not go in.

5. Revising the cards or documents of all the participants in the game under the referee's supervision.

# Rule VII. Duration of the Match

1. A match lasts forty minutes. It is divided into two halves of twenty minutes each with a half-time break of ten minutes.

Once time expires, each of the halves continues in order to allow the execution of a maximum foul or a free kick without a wall of players.

2. The coaches and the captains of each team can request two one-minute time-outs, one per half. In order to request a time-out, the ball must not be in play.

3. The appropriate associations will only change the duration of the matches and of the halftime break as an exceptional measure and generally only for reasons related to the broadcasting of televised matches.

# Rule VIII. Kickoffs

## 1. Starting the Game, Initial Kickoff

(a) The winner of a coin flip chooses the side of the field or whether to kick off. The losing team makes the other choice.

(b) The match starts with a kickoff after a signal from the referee. One player kicks the ball from the center of the field towards the other side of the field.

(c) All players must be on their own side of the field. The opponents must be outside the 10-foot (3-m) radius circle at the center of the field before the ball starts to move.

(d) The ball is in play as soon as it is no longer in contact with the foot or hands of the player who makes a throw-in or who kicks off. However, the rules include some exceptions.

(e) The player who kicks off

cannot touch the ball again until another player has touched it.

(f) No goals may be scored directly from an initial kickoff.

## 2. After Scoring a Goal

The game restarts with a kickoff by a player from the team that did not score.

## 3. After Halftime

The teams switch sides, and the team that did not kickoff at the beginning of the match kicks off at the beginning of the second half.

## Penalty

In case of infraction of items 1, 2, and 3 of this rule, the team repeats the kickoff, unless the player who kicked off touched it before another player did. In that case, the ball goes to the other team, and they will make a throw-in from the touchline at the point where the foul occurred.

## 4. After Temporary Interruptions

(a) To restart the match after an interruption other than the ones mentioned in the rules, as long as the ball has not left the playing area immediately before the interruption, the referee will drop the ball on the floor where it was before the interruption (assuming it was on the playing area immediately before the interruption), unless the ball was in the penalty area. In that case, the ball starts on the line closest to where it was when play was interrupted.

(b) In this case, the ball is in play from the moment it touches the floor. If the ball leaves the playing area before a player touches it, the referee must drop it again. None of the players may play the ball before it touches the floor. If anyone does, the referee will drop it again.

# Rule IX. Ball in Play

1. The ball will be out of play when:

(a) The ball has completely crossed a touchline or goal line, either on the floor or in the air.

(b) The referee has stopped the game.

(c) The ball has hit the ceiling of the arena after a cleared ball or other action. In this case, the ball will go back in play with a throw-in by the other team from the closest point to where it hit the ceiling.

2. The ball is in play from the beginning to the end of the game in all other cases, even in the following situations:

(a) If it returns to the playing area after bouncing off one of the goalposts.

(b) If it returns to the playing area after touching a referee who was inside the playing area.

(c) Until the referee reaches a decision regarding a potential infraction of the rules.

3. Lines are part of the area they define. Therefore, the goal lines and touchlines are a part of the playing area.

## Rule X. Scoring

1. Except in cases described in these rules, a team scores a goal when the ball has completely crossed the goal line between the vertical posts and under the horizontal post of the goal without being touched by an attacking player's hand.

2. The team that has scored the most points wins the game. If neither side scores, or if both teams score the same amount of goals, the result is a tie.

## Rule XI. Throw-in

1. When the ball crosses the touchlines, either on the ground or in the air, a throw-in is necessary to continue play. A player of the team that did not touch the ball last makes the throw-in from the exact place where the ball left the playing area. The ball can go in any direction.

2. The player who makes the throw-in must face the playing area with a part of both feet touching the ground from the outside of the touchline. He must use both hands and throw the ball forward from behind his head. His feet must be perpendicular to the touchline.

3. The ball will be in play after the throw-in.

The player who makes the throw-in cannot touch the ball again until another player touches or plays it.

4. A goal scored directly from a throw-in or a goal resulting from a throw-in towards the opponent's area will not be valid unless another player (except the goalie) has touched the ball.

*Penalties*

(a) If the throw-in is not executed properly, the ball goes to the other team for a throw-in.

(b) If a player makes a throw-in from a position other than where the ball exited the field, the ball goes to the other team for a throw-in.

(c) If the player does not make the throw-in within five seconds after he receives the ball, the ball goes to the other team for a throw-in.

(d) If the ball goes into the goal from a throw-in without another player having touched it, the team receives a goal kick.

(e) If the ball goes into the goal from a throw-in after only the goalie has touched it, the attacking team will have a corner kick from the place closest to where the ball entered the goal.

(f) If a player makes the throw-in in the direction of his own goal and the ball goes into the goal without another player touching it, the other team will have a corner kick from the place closest to where the ball entered the goal.

(g) If a player makes the throw-in towards his own goal and any other player touches the ball, including the goalie, before the ball goes into the goal, the goal is valid.

## Rule XII. Corner Kick

1. When the ball completely crosses the goal line (unless a goal has been scored on the ground or in the air) after being touched last by a defensive player, the other team gets a corner kick.

2. The corner kick is for the offensive team. The player must use both hands and place the ball behind his head, throwing it forward. Part of his feet must be on the ground, outside the playing area, and the player should be facing the angle formed by the touchline and goal line, at the point where they converge.

3. A goal resulting from a corner kick is not valid unless a player other than the goalie touches the ball.

*Penalties*

(a) If the corner kick has been incorrectly performed, the opponent will have the right to a goal throw.

(b) If the corner kick is not performed with five seconds after the player has received the ball, the opponent will have the right to a side throw.

(c) If the ball crosses the goal line directly after a corner kick has only been touched by the goalie, the goal is invalid and the team will have another corner kick, this time from the closest point to where the ball crossed the goal line.

## Rule XIII. Goal Throw

1. When the ball has completely crossed the end line, excluding the goal itself, either on the ground or in the air, and being touched last by a player of the offensive team, there will be a goal throw.

2. The goal throw will be made by the goalie, only with his hands and from inside the penalty area.

3. The goal throw will be considered correct when the ball has cleared the penalty area. The opponent must remain outside of the penalty area until the ball

133

is in play.

### Penalties

(a) If the ball crosses the center line without having been touched by a player and without touching the ground, the referee will award a free kick to the opposite team from the place on the center line where the ball crossed the field.

(b) If a teammate of the goalie kicks or touches the goal kick or if an opponent kicks or touches the ball inside the penalty area, the goal kick must be replayed.

# Rule XIV. Fouls and Infractions

### 1. Technical Fouls

The following are technical fouls:

(a) Kicking (or attempting to kick) the opponent.

(b) Tripping the opponent, making the opponent fall, or trying to make the opponent fall whether tripping him in the calf or falling in front or behind him.

(c) Jumping or throwing oneself over an opponent.

(d) Violently or dangerously charging an opponent.

(e) Charging an opponent from behind when the opponent is not obstructive.

(f) Hitting or trying to hit an opponent; or spitting at an opponent.

(g) Holding an opponent to prevent him from playing.

(h) Pushing an opponent with the hands or arms.

(i) Charging an opponent with the shoulder when the ball is not at issue.

(j) Playing the ball by taking it, hitting it, or throwing it with the hands or arms, except when the goalie does this inside the penalty area.

### Penalties

(a) The referee will award a free kick to the opponent from the point where the infraction occurred, except when applying the rule of advantage. In that case, the referee will mark the cumulative foul after the play is over. If he considers the infraction to be dangerous or intentional, he shows a yellow or blue card.

(b) If a defensive player makes one of these two fouls within his defense area (20 feet [6 m]), the penalty will be a penalty shot.

### The Following Are Also Technical Fouls:

(k) Playing dangerously, for example, taking the ball from the goalie's hands

(l) Intentionally obstructing

an opponent without playing the ball, for example, running between the opponent and the ball

(m) Raising the feet to kick using a bicycle movement or kicking the ball without any intention of playing it, and kicking an opponent or almost kicking him instead

(n) Charging the goalie, unless he is out of his area

As goalie, receiving the ball from a teammate, when putting the ball back in play (with hands or feet), until an opponent touches or plays the ball.

If the goalie touches the ball or the ball touches him, even accidentally, the referee will consider the ball back in play and will consider the touch as a pass from the goalie to one of his teammates.

(o) The goalie's intervention in any play outside the goal area. The infraction occurs when he touches the ball or an opponent outside the goal area, thus taking part in the play or obstructing the play

(p) When the goalie throws or kicks the ball and no other player touches it and the ball does not touch the ground in that half of the playing area. In all other cases, the game continues without penalty

(q) Deliberately wasting time,

such as passing back and forth to kill time (passive play)

(r) Using dangerous play, such as hitting with the soles, lifting the feet to chest height, etc.

### Penalties

(a) The opponents will receive a free kick where the foul took place, unless the referee applies the rule of advantage.

(b) If the infraction was inside the playing area, the foul will be shot from the 10-foot (6 m) line, at the place closest to where the infraction took place.

### 2. Personal Fouls

The following are personal fouls:

(a) When the goalie slows down the game for more than five seconds by holding the ball in his area instead of playing it.

(b) When a player obstructs a play by holding the ball with his feet or preventing it from moving with his body, except for when the goalie is on the ground in his area.

(c) When the player who throws in the ball or makes a corner, free, or penalty kick touches the ball before any other player can.

(d) Slowing down the game more than five seconds by getting ready for a free, penalty, or corner kick, or a throw-in or goal kick.

(e) When a player without the required attire touches a ball that is in play.

(f) Using words to confuse the opponent.

(g) Goalies may play, roll, bounce, and touch the ball as many times as they need to in their area, but only within the five-second limit.

(h) Retaining the ball in a team's own goal area for more than five seconds when the ball is in play.

## Penalties

(a) The referee penalizes all of these infractions by awarding the opponent a throw-in from the point closest to where the infraction took place.

(b) In the case described in h, the referee will penalize the player who touched the ball last at the end of the time limit.

## 3. Players' Disciplinary Fouls

The following infractions are disciplinary fouls:

1. During substitutions, entering the field before the player to be replaced has left the field or entering the field in an inappropriate place.

2. Showing through words or actions disapproval of the referee's decisions.

3. Persistently breaking the rules of the game.

4. Incorrect behavior.

5. Changing the number on a jersey without previously telling the referees.

6. Addressing the referees or spectators to argue a decision.

7. Taking more than five seconds in the kickoffs from center field.

## 4. Coaches' and Trainers' Fouls

1. Entering the field to give instructions to the players or helping them when injured without authorization from the referee.

Coaches and trainers must remain outside the playing area. They can move about as long as they do not obstruct the timekeeper's view of the game.

2. Addressing the referees, opponents, or spectators disrespectfully.

## Penalties

(a) The referee penalizes a player committing a disciplinary foul with a card, and if he commits the same foul again, the referee will disqualify him or permanently expel him from the game.

(b) When a game stops because of a penalty, disqualification, or expulsion, the referee starts it again with a neutral drop of the ball at the point closest to where the infraction took place.

(c) Interrupting the game must never benefit the team that committed the foul. If that occurs, the referee must let the game continue and assign a penalty once the play is over.

(d) A referee can expel a player if the referee feels:

1. A player exhibits violent behavior.

2. A player is too rough.

3. A player displays insulting or obscene behavior.

4. A player reacts with actions or words to a foul.

(e) When the referee interrupts the game to disqualify or expel a player and no other infraction like those described in these rules has occurred, the referee restarts the game with a neutral drop of the ball at the place closest to where the infraction occurred.

# Rule XV.

## Cumulative Fouls

1. All technical and personal fouls described in Rule XIV are CUMULATIVE FOULS.

The referees must enter all cumulative fouls in the record of the match. This applies to both team fouls and individual fouls.

2. Technical fouls will result in a free penalty kick. If a team scores a goal as a result of the free kick, the goal is valid. The referee can let the game continue if the situation benefits the team that was fouled. The referee penalizes personal fouls with a throw-in.

3. Each of the teams may incur five cumulative fouls in each half with the right to form a defensive wall.

4. When a foul results in a free penalty kick with a defensive wall, the referee shall direct matters with his whistle. The player will then have five seconds to kick the ball or request that the wall maintain the proper distance.

5. In a free kick, no player from the defensive wall can be closer than 16 feet (5 m) to the ball until the ball is in play.

If an opponent does not respect the distance before the kick, the referee must delay the kick until the player moves. After this additional infraction, the referee may warn the player, show him a card, and even disqualify him from the match if he repeats it.

6. In the event that the defensive team has a free kick inside its own goal area, the goalie may

not pick up the ball with his hands. A player must kick the ball out of the goal area or the kick will be replayed and the player who made the infraction will receive a warning.

7. The table referee will raise signs numbered from one to five as teams make cumulative fouls.

When a team makes its fifth cumulative foul, the table referee will tell the referee and place a flag or other sign on the side of the table that the team is defending, no matter where the team's bench is.

8. From the sixth cumulative foul on, all penalty kicks will take place at the spot where the foul took place, and the other side may not use defensive walls.

9. The restricted area is the inside surface of the triangle formed by the lines between the ball and the points of intersection of the goal line and the area line.

10. When a player is making a kick, all the other players except the goalie must stay clear of the restricted zone and outside the area. The defense must be at least 16 feet (5 m) from the ball. They cannot be in the way of the player who is making the kick or in any way prevent him from kicking.

11. When the ball is in play

after a free kick without a wall, all players may enter the restricted area.

*Penalties*

(a) Any player—attacker or defender—who enters the restricted area after the referee has blown his whistle and before the ball is in play will receive a yellow card.

(b) If a defender commits an infraction and the other team scores a goal, the goal is valid and the defender will receive a yellow card.

(c) If an attacker commits the infraction and scores a goal, the goal is not valid. A goal kick will follow.

(d) If a player makes a free kick (without a defensive wall) towards the opposite goal area and a teammate receives the ball, the game stops. The player who made the free kick receives a yellow card, and the opponents get a free kick.

(e) If a player makes a free kick (without a defensive wall) towards the opposite goal area and an attacker enters the goal area after the ball, he will not be able to score the goal by directly receiving the ball from the kick.

# Rule XVI. Penalty

1. A penalty kick is a direct kick 20 feet (6 m) from the goal. All

players except the goalie and the player who kicks the ball are inside the field but outside the penalty area and at least 16 feet (5 m) behind the ball in an imaginary line parallel to the goal.

2. The other team's goalie must remain on his goal line between the goalposts without moving his feet until the ball is in play again.

3. The player who kicks the penalty must kick the ball forward only once, and he may not play it again until another player has touched it or played it.

4. The ball will be in play once it is no longer in contact with the foot of the player who kicks the penalty.

# Referee's Signals

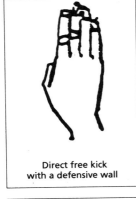

Direct free kick
with a defensive wall

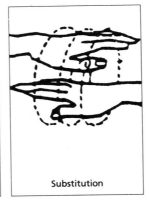

Substitution

Four fouls

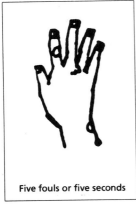

Five fouls or five seconds

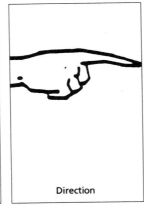

Direction

Time-out

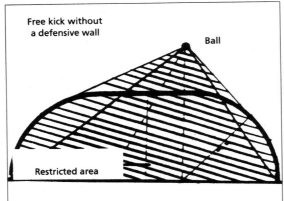

Free kick without
a defensive wall

Ball

Restricted area

End of first or second half

# Index